PRAISE FOR KERI-RAE BARNUM'S

Tough Love for Indie Authors

"Engaging, accessible, and easy to digest...I wish this had been available when I was starting out. Unlike so many 'expert advice' books on self-publishing, this one is backed by someone who actually knows what they're doing."

—Barbara Hinske, *USA Today* Bestselling Indie Author

• • •

"When Keri-Rae Barnum promises, she delivers. *Tough Love for Indie Authors* left me feeling empowered and self-confident in my journey as an author."

—Elle Mott, Creative Nonfiction Author and Resource Sharing Adviser, Cincinnati & Hamilton County Public Library

Sibylline Press

Published in the United States by Sibylline Press,
an imprint of All Things Book LLC, California.

Sibylline Press is dedicated to publishing
the brilliant work of women authors ages 50 and older.
www.sibyllinepress.com

Ebook ISBN: 9798897400072
Print ISBN: 9798897400065
Library of Congress Control Number: 2025934312

Cover Design & Book Production: Alicia Feltman

Sibylline
PRESS

Tough Love

for INDIE AUTHORS

An Honest Look at What it Takes to
Win in Self-Publishing

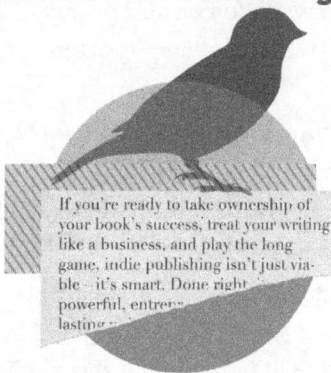

If you're ready to take ownership of your book's success, treat your writing like a business, and play the long game, indie publishing isn't just viable — it's smart. Done right powerful, entre~~ lasting ~~

KERI-RAE BARNUM
Foreword by AMY COLLINS

Sibylline
PRESS

AN IMPRINT OF ALL THINGS BOOK

Table of Contents

Foreword

Here's the thing no one tells you when you first decide to publish a book: there will be at least one moment when you find yourself curled up in the fetal position wondering why you thought this was a good idea. For me, that moment came the day I accidentally approved a title page where the author's name was misspelled. Twenty-five thousand copies were printed with the author's name wrong. Nine people looked it over. We all said, "Yep! That looks great."

Welcome to publishing.

I've been working in books for over three decades now—first as a book buyer for a chain of stores in New York. Then as a sales rep and Sales Director for a big publishing house. Then fifteen years helping indie authors make good decisions. And now as a literary agent.

I have seen the sausage made from every possible angle. I've helped launch bestsellers with the biggest publishers in the world and I've held the hands of indie authors when they realized that they could quit their day job. I've watched writers build six- and seven-figure careers from their kitchen tables. And I've personally witnessed authors sabotage themselves with more conviction than a toddler trying to "help" bake a cake.

So when Keri-Rae Barnum told me she was going to write this book, we talked about all the annoying books out there that spit out chirpy pep talks about "living your dream." She didn't want to write that book. She wanted to tell the truth.

Because no matter which path you take—traditional or indie—success in publishing isn't about luck, fate, or the perfect font choice. It's about strategy, mindset, and treating your career like a business.

And if you're reading this foreword, chances are you're the kind of person who wants to do exactly that.

Indie publishing is hard. It's thrilling, empowering, and often more profitable than traditional publishing, yes. But it's also hard.

There's no built-in team. No marketing department sending your book to Trevor Noah. No publicist chasing down reviews while you casually sip coffee in a sun-drenched writing nook. (I've never had that nook. If you have, please know I'm jealous.)

But it is absolutely possible to thrive as an indie author if you're willing to show up and do the work. And I've seen it happen—over and over again.

I think of Hazel Mack, one of the most inspiring indie authors I've had the privilege to work with. Hazel didn't just write great books; she built a business around them. She studied her readers like a sociologist with a romance habit. She figured out how to get her books directly into readers' hands, how to keep them coming back, and—this part is key—how to show up like a professional every single day. Hazel didn't wait for permission or praise. She showed up with grit and grace, launched one book after another, and turned her author career into a revenue stream that most small presses would envy.

Or Elizabeth Stephens, whose spicy, genre-bending romances are as bold as she is. Elizabeth didn't fit neatly into traditional boxes. She wrote stories that defied market assumptions—about race, about genre, about who gets to be center stage—and guess what? Her readers found her anyway. Her career is proof that when you trust your voice and show up with persistence, self-publishing sometimes offers creative freedom that traditional publishing can't touch.

Both of these women taught me something critical: self-publishing isn't about settling. It's about owning. It's about looking at your career and saying, "This is mine, and I'm going to build it like it matters."

They looked at both traditional and indie publishing and said, "I want to do this myself." It wasn't that they couldn't get a traditional deal, they didn't want one.

(Spoiler: they both have traditional deals now ... but only as a side gig to see what would happen. They will be indie publishing forever.)

Now, I'm not here to bash traditional publishing. I believe in it. I am an agent for heaven's sake. Traditional publishing is my paycheck. And there are some books that need the distribution power, the legacy clout, and the infrastructure that traditional publishing can offer. But there's a difference between recognizing those benefits and romanticizing the system like it's some kind of literary wonderland.

The truth is, traditional publishing is slower. It's less flexible. And unless you're a breakout name, you'll be doing most of your own marketing anyway—often while giving up control over your title, your cover, and sometimes even your ending. I've seen authors get six-figure advances and not earn out. I've seen midlist darlings dropped without warning. I've seen more than one author cry in a hotel lobby at a book conference when they realized the machine they worked so hard to get into ... wasn't really built for them.

But I've also seen indie authors cry happy tears when they hit their first 10,000 sales. When they quit their day job. When a foreign publisher comes calling because their book blew up on TikTok. (Keri is going to tell you that virality isn't a strategy—and it isn't—but it still makes for a nice Tuesday when it happens.)

So what's the point? The point is that both paths can work. Both have merit. Both have potholes.

And this book is the roadmap I wish every author had before they started driving.

Inside these pages, you'll find practical advice—like how to build a team, how to market your book without hating yourself, how to price and position your product like the professional you are.

But more than that, you'll find permission. Permission to take your work seriously. To invest in yourself. To treat this career like it matters—because it does.

Keri wrote this book for the author who's sick of guessing. Who's tired of wondering why their book isn't selling. Who's ready to stop dabbling and start building.

It's not about chasing validation. It's about creating a plan.

So welcome. Glad you're here. But don't expect sugarcoating.

Keri is going to tell you what works, what doesn't, and what's worth spending your time and money on. This book will tell the truth, even when it stings. And then it will help you move forward.

You've got this. We've got your back.

Now get to work.

Amy Collins

Introduction

Anyone can publish a book today. The barriers to entry have been obliterated. You don't need an agent. You don't need a publishing deal. You can write a book, format it, upload it, and be "published" within hours.

But here's the thing: That's not the same as publishing well.

Publishing well: creating a book that sells, earns fans, builds your brand, and contributes to a sustainable author career, is a whole different game. And far too many writers don't know the rules.

That's why I wrote this book.

I'm not here to tell you it's easy or that success is just one viral TikTok away. What I am here to do is give you the straight truth about the industry, the process, the pitfalls, and the work it actually takes to publish well.

It's not all doom and gloom. There are real opportunities for authors who treat this like a profession. There are thousands of success stories of authors who have built full-time careers, hit bestseller lists, landed traditional deals on their terms, and reached readers around the world.

You can be one of them.

But not by accident. Not by following bad advice from the

internet. And not by treating publishing like a hobby.

This is your career. This is your business. And I'm here to help you treat it that way.

If you're ready to take ownership of your book's success, treat your writing like a business, and play the long game, indie publishing isn't just viable—it's smart. Done right, it can be a powerful, entrepreneurial path to a lasting writing career.

Inside these pages, you'll find:

- Hard-earned wisdom from industry insiders

- Case studies of successful independent authors

- Clear, actionable strategies (with no fluff)

- Tough love about what it really takes to succeed

- Encouragement (yes, even when I am being blunt)

Whether you're just starting out or trying to figure out why your last book flopped, this book will meet you where you are—and help you level up.

Let's dive in.

PART I

*To Be or Not To Be
...A Publisher*

CHAPTER 1

Publishing Paths: Choose Your Road

So, you've written a book. Or maybe you've skipped ahead even though you're still staring at a blinking cursor, wondering if a title and an epigraph count as "progress." Either way, you've reached the same fork in the road every aspiring author eventually faces:

How do I publish this thing?

The good news: there are more options than ever.

The bad news: there are more options than ever.

Back in the day, your path was more or less carved in stone. You'd finish your manuscript, send out query letters, cross your fingers, and pray that someone—*anyone*—in publishing would say, "Yes." If you beat the odds, your book might see a bookstore shelf within a couple of years.

Today, the publishing landscape has evolved. Authors now have several viable paths to bring their books to market.

- Traditional Publishing
- Hybrid Publishing
- Self-Publishing (Indie Publishing)

Each path leads to the same destination—a published book—but the roads are drastically different. None of these paths are inherently better or worse; they're just different. Each comes with its own balance of creative control, professional support, upfront investment, timeline, and potential rewards.

This chapter is not about telling you which road to take. It's about helping you make a fully informed decision, based on facts (not fantasy.) Because whichever option you choose, you need to go into it with your eyes wide open and a solid plan in place.

Path #1: Traditional Publishing

This is the route most of us grew up romanticizing. You write a brilliant manuscript, land a literary agent, sign with a Big 5 publisher, and bask in the glow of your book tour and morning show appearances. Your only job? Write.

Now let's snap out of that dream and get real.

Traditional publishing often means months (or years) spent querying agents, revising your manuscript based on rejection letters, and waiting. If you do land a deal, it could take another 18 to 24 months before your book hits the shelves. Yes, the publisher handles editing, design, and distribution. But you? You'll still be on the hook for most of the marketing.

And control? Let's just say it's not in your hands. You likely won't get the final say on your cover, price point, or how your book is promoted. Royalties are typically 7–12% on print and 25% on digital, after you've earned out any advance—assuming you get one.

Still, for many authors, traditional publishing is a solid choice. If you prefer writing to wrangling metadata, and if the idea of handling your own book production makes your eyes twitch, this path can offer real value.

Just don't mistake it for a fairy tale.

Path #2: Hybrid Publishing

Hybrid publishing promises the best of both worlds ... and sometimes delivers it. I have seen hybrid models evolve into meaningful partnerships that produce beautiful books and long-term success. But I have also seen them crash hard, delivering disappointment disguised in a glossy sales pitch.

Here's how it works: you pay a publisher to help produce your book. Sometimes this is one lump sum, but more often it's a combination of a specific dollar amount and a percentage of royalties. In return for payment, the publisher offers editing, design, production, and distribution. Sometimes they also include marketing, although this may come at an upcharge.

Some hybrid publishers operate like boutique presses and provide real value. Others are glorified vanity presses charging authors thousands of dollars for services they don't need and exposure they'll never get.

If you're considering the hybrid publishing route, ask the tough questions:

- Does this publisher have a strong track record and solid reviews?
- What exactly am I paying for?
- Who owns the rights to my book?
- How are royalties split?
- Will my book be marketed and distributed outside of Amazon?
- Do they have successful titles in my genre?
- What do their authors say?
- Are their other authors happy? Are their books visible?
- Are they selling beyond their inner circles?

11

Too many authors dive into hybrid deals without understanding what they're buying. If you're paying thousands of dollars for a subpar product and still doing all your own marketing, you might be better off self-publishing and keeping full control.

Path #3: Self-Publishing (Indie Publishing)

Once dismissed as the last resort for rejected writers, self-publishing has transformed into a legitimate, scalable, and often profitable model. It's no longer the wild west; it's an entire ecosystem. And when done right, it can be every bit as professional and, in many cases, more profitable than the traditional route.

Throughout this book, I will be using the terms "self-publishing," "independent publishing," and "indie publishing" interchangeably. All three describe the same thing: an author who takes full ownership of publishing their own book. While some hybrid publishers use the term "self-publishing," true self-publishing happens when the author takes off their writer hat and puts on their publisher hat.

In this model, you are the publisher. You make every decision. You choose your editors, cover designers, and formatters. You control the timeline, the pricing, the marketing, and the metadata (yes, that's a thing). You also keep more of the profits—up to 70% on eBooks sold through Amazon and other retailers.

Sound amazing? It is. But also ... it's a ton of work.

You're investing your own money upfront. You're coordinating professionals. You're building your author brand and marketing your book like it's a product launch. You're not just a writer anymore. You're also a creative director, marketing strategist, and CEO all rolled into one.

Self-publishing might be right for you if:

- You want full control over your publishing process.

- You are willing to invest time and money upfront.

- You have a strong vision for your book and brand.

- You want to move fast and build momentum.

- You are self-motivated.

- You are willing to tackle tasks outside your comfort zone.

There's no fairy god-publisher here. Just you, a lot of decisions, and a steep—but manageable—learning curve. Done right, self-publishing is not just a viable option; it's a professional and strategic one.

What Indie Isn't ... and What to Watch Out For

It's time for a heart-to-heart. Some authors approach self-publishing with these arguments:

- "My book is perfect and doesn't need editing." (It's not. It does.)

- "I'm a perfectionist and need total control." (Cool. Just be prepared to also control your cover, metadata, ad strategy, printer setup, ISBN management, email marketing ...)

- "I can make more money per book." (True. But can you sell enough books to matter?)

Control is a wonderful thing ... right up until it turns into a DIY disaster. This is publishing, not a Pinterest craft night. Yes, having creative control is empowering, but it only works when you know when to call in the pros.

Self-publishing isn't:

- Uploading a rough draft with a Canva cover and hoping it sells
- Skipping editing because "your friend has good grammar"
- Doing zero marketing and expecting magic

Self-publishing isn't a shortcut. It's a professional publishing model that takes time, money, and commitment.

What Indie *Is* ... And Why It Might Be for You

Here's where self-publishing shines:

- You already have a platform or business and want to deliver a book to your audience.
- You're ready to move fast and don't want to wait years to publish.
- You want to test the market, build leverage for a future traditional deal, or start your own publishing imprint.
- You want to make your own rules ... and are ready to follow through with the work it takes to make it successful.
- You have mapped out multiple future titles and are dedicated to publishing on a regular schedule.

If that sounds like you, congratulations! You're not just a writer. You're a publisher in the making.

Don't Let This Choice Paralyze You

It's easy to get stuck in research mode, bouncing between blog posts, videos, and advice from every corner of the internet. But indecision kills momentum. The most successful authors don't wait until they feel "ready." They make informed choices, commit, and get moving. If you're leaning indie, trust yourself. You've got this.

Feature	Traditional Publishing	Hybrid Publishing	Self-Publishing (Indie)
Cost to Author	$0 upfront (publisher pays)	$$-$$$$ (you pay for services)	$$-$$$ (you hire your own team)
Time to Market	18–36 months	6–12 months	2–6 months
Creative Control	Low	Medium	High
Royalties	7–12% print, 25% digital	Varies but usually higher than traditional	Up to 50-60% print, up to 70% digital
Marketing Support	Basic unless you're a big name	Minimal or limited	100% your responsibility
Distribution Reach	Strong (retail, library)	Varies but usually online only	Online + direct or traditional if you expand
Prestige/ Perception	High	Mixed	Growing
Best For	Authors who want infrastructure	Authors who want support + input	Authors seeking control + high ROI

So ... Which Path Is Right for You?

That depends on your goals, resources, and personality.

If you want to hand off the business side, are hoping for big deals, seek prestige, and have time to wait, traditional may be for you. If you want a professional, done-for-you experience for a single book (or one every few years) and don't mind paying for it, a vetted hybrid press could be a fit. If you're ready to own your publishing journey, take the risks, and reap the rewards, indie publishing is your lane. It's all about aligning your goals with your publishing path and planning accordingly. This book, for example, was traditionally published despite my strong background in and connection to indie publishing. Why? Because I recognized that this particular work would be best supported by collaborating with Sibylline Press. Our goals aligned: I wanted broad distribution, professional partnership, and a mission-driven press that could magnify the message in these pages.

I recognize that every publishing path comes with its own set of pros and cons. I am not here to speak badly about any of them. What I *am* here to do is offer a brutally honest look at what each path truly demands—and show you how to succeed, whichever one you choose.

That said, I believe in indie publishing. And if you're holding this book, chances are you're leaning that way too.

If you're nodding along, but still second-guessing yourself, this quick gut check will help you decide if you're really ready to go indie.

Self-Publishing Readiness Checklist

Ask yourself:

- Am I willing to invest time learning the publishing business?
- Can I afford to pay for editing, design, and production?
- Do I have (or am I willing to build) a platform?
- Can I make decisions and manage a team?
- Am I prepared to handle marketing, ads, and reader outreach?
- Do I understand that this is a long-term business, not a one-time project?

Still wondering if self-publishing is too risky or fringe? You're in good company because one of America's most iconic authors once asked the same question.

CASE STUDY: MARK TWAIN

Self-Publishing Before It Was Cool

Long before Kindle Direct Publishing or print-on-demand, Samuel Clemens (better known as Mark Twain) became one of the earliest examples of a wildly successful self-published author.

Twain had already achieved fame with *The Adventures of Tom Sawyer*, which was published traditionally. But when it came time to release *Adventures of Huckleberry Finn*, he wanted more control and a bigger slice of the profits. So, in 1884, he launched his own publishing company: Charles L. Webster and Company, named after his nephew and business partner.

Through that company, Twain published *Huck Finn* himself. The gamble paid off.

By self-publishing, Twain was able to:

- Retain creative control over every aspect of the book
- Earn significantly more money than he would have through a traditional publisher
- Pioneer new distribution strategies, including subscription sales and door-to-door agents (the 19th-century version of direct-to-reader marketing)

But Twain didn't stop with his own work. His publishing house also released *Personal Memoirs of Ulysses S. Grant*, a massive commercial success, with over 300,000 copies sold and an enduring legacy in American nonfiction.

Of course, it wasn't all smooth sailing. Twain's company eventually collapsed under the weight of less successful titles and risky investments. But that doesn't diminish the fact that Twain was an early trailblazer in author-led publishing. He saw the upside of owning his publishing process ... and he took it.

He wasn't chasing indie status out of desperation. He was claiming his stake in the business side of authorship. And if that sounds familiar, it should.

Today's indie authors have access to tools and distribution channels Twain could never have imagined. But the core idea remains the same: take ownership of your work, treat it like a business, and reach readers on your own terms.

Twain didn't choose self-publishing out of necessity. He chose it because it made strategic sense.

If you're leaning toward indie publishing, you're in excellent company. You're not settling. You're stepping into a tradition of authors who believed their books—and their careers—were worth building independently.

Because here's the truth: self-publishing isn't a fallback. It's a power move.

CHAPTER 2

Why Indie Is a Power Move

Self-publishing is not what you do when you "fail" at traditional publishing. It's what you do when you want ownership, speed, leverage, and full control over your author career. It's what you do when you want to connect directly with your readers and fans. Choosing the indie path is not a compromise, it's a strategy.

There's a persistent narrative that indie authors are just writers who couldn't make it the "real" way. That's outdated—and wrong. Some of today's top-earning authors are indie or started out that way. Not because they had no other choice, but because they saw the business potential and took it seriously. They understood that self-publishing allows for rapid idea testing, direct marketing, and the ability to build a loyal reader base on their own terms.

Authors like Amy Pennza, Hazel Mack, and Lexi Foss are pulling in high six-figure incomes from indie publishing, and they're far from the only ones.

They didn't wait for someone else to give them approval. They didn't hope someone else would launch their career. They took action and earned their success. Not by accident. Not by luck. But by learning the business of publishing and stepping into the role of CEO.

Indie Publishing Myths to Burn Now

- "Indie authors can't get into bookstores." (False. You can, with the right tools. But it *is* one of the hardest parts of indie publishing.)

- "Self-publishing is easy money." (Nope. It's a business.)

- "You have to go viral to succeed." (Wrong. Consistency outperforms luck 99% of the time.)

Indie Success Stories Aren't Unicorns

It's tempting to believe that "real" success only comes from a New York publisher. But the truth is, indie success comes in many forms:

- The romance author who built a six-figure income from direct reader relationships.

- The nonfiction expert who uses books to drive business leads and speaking gigs.

- The fantasy writer whose serialized fiction took off online—and who now earns more writing than in their day job.

As you'll see in the coming pages, these aren't rare exceptions. They're increasingly common outcomes when an author treats publishing like a profession, not a hobby.

Indie authors can and *do*:

- Hit bestseller lists
- Land traditional publishing and foreign rights deals
- Get film and TV options
- Build full-time careers on their own terms

And perhaps most importantly? Indie authors don't wait for permission. They take control of their own destiny and publish with purpose.

Speed and Agility: The Indie Edge

In traditional publishing, it can take two to three years to get a book on shelves. In the indie world you can write, produce, and launch a professional-quality book in six months or even less.

That speed is powerful. It allows indie authors to:

- Respond to market trends in real time
- Launch multiple books in a year
- Pivot quickly when something isn't working

When you go indie, you're not stuck waiting on a marketing department or a release calendar. You're in the driver's seat.

CASE STUDY: ELANA JOHNSON

Scaling Success with Speed and Strategy

If anyone proves that indie publishing rewards speed, strategy, and reader connection, it's Elana Johnson.

Writing under multiple pen names—including Liz Isaacson, Jessie Newton, and Donna Jeffries—Johnson has authored over 160 books spanning clean romance, inspirational fiction, and contemporary women's fiction. And she hasn't just written fast, she's published fast, with new titles often dropping every four to six weeks.

Traditional publishing? It couldn't have kept up.

Indie publishing didn't just accommodate Johnson's pace, it empowered her to turn that speed into a sustainable, scalable career.

And this wasn't about churning out books for the sake of volume. Johnson writes with intention. She understands her readers, studies the market, and plans release schedules around audience expectations. When a book or series gains traction, she leans in—doubling down on what's working. If something underperforms, she pivots without waiting 18 months for approval or a new slot on a traditional release calendar.

The Indie Advantage: Agility and Ownership

Johnson controls her schedule, production, branding, and marketing. That means no gatekeepers and no waiting games. Just clear decisions, fast execution, and direct feedback from readers.

She operates her own publishing imprint, AEJ Creative Works, and teaches other authors how to build rapid-release strategies through her *Writing and Releasing Rapidly* guidebook and online communities. Her business model is a blend of craft and commerce, powered by consistency and deep market awareness.

Results That Compound

Elana Johnson's success isn't an accident. It's a case study in professional self-publishing:

- **Consistent output** that keeps her frontlist and backlist selling

- **Deep reader engagement** through newsletters, Facebook groups, and social media

- **Control over all publishing decisions,** from genre branding to metadata

- **Multiple income streams** via direct sales, eBook platforms, and paperback sales

Most importantly, she's built a career that runs on *her* terms. Indie publishing didn't just let Elana Johnson go fast. It let her build a thriving business by responding to her market in real time—something traditional publishing simply can't match.

Her story is a reminder that success in indie publishing isn't just about writing fast. It's about writing smart, releasing strategically, and treating your author business like … well, a business.

Creative Freedom: Your Book, Your Way

Traditional publishers are businesses. They make decisions based on risk, return, and how well a book fits into established commercial categories. If your book doesn't follow a proven formula—or it blends genres in unconventional ways—it might get passed over, no matter how compelling the writing.

That's where indie-publishing shines.

As an indie author, you don't need to wait for a publisher to write what excites you. You can:

- Blend genres
- Experiment with tone and format
- Choose your own cover and pricing
- Release on your schedule, not someone else's

Creative freedom doesn't mean ignoring professional standards (we'll cover those), but it does mean your vision leads. And sometimes, that freedom pays off in ways traditional publishing couldn't predict.

Here's one author who proved it.

CASE STUDY: MATT DINNIMAN

Building a Breakout Series on His Own Terms

Matt Dinniman launched his *Dungeon Crawler Carl* series as an independently published project. The books, a blend of LitRPG, dark humor, and horror—complete with a talking cat sidekick—didn't follow traditional genre conventions. But readers loved them.

By self-publishing, Dinniman maintained full creative control, releasing books that were uniquely his. He built a massive fanbase and gained particular traction in the audiobook market, where the series became a cult favorite.

In 2024, that success led to a major publishing deal: Ace Books, an imprint of Penguin Random House, acquired

North American print rights to the first six books in the series. Dinniman retained control of the digital editions, allowing him to expand his reach while keeping the independence that helped him succeed.

Matt Dinniman didn't wait for a gatekeeper. He wrote the books he wanted to read, proved their value directly to an audience, and turned that momentum into a hybrid publishing win.

Self-publishing doesn't mean going it alone. It means going first—trusting your voice, engaging your audience, and building a career that reflects your creative vision. And sometimes, just like Dinniman, it means getting the best of both worlds.

Building Leverage: Indie Is Just the Start

A well-executed self-published book can lead to traditional publishing deals, foreign rights sales, and even film or TV options. But none of that happens by accident.

Many indie authors use their books to build leverage. A successful indie launch can open doors to:

- Agent representation
- Traditional deals on your terms
- Translation and foreign rights
- Licensing and merchandising opportunities

I know firsthand that publishers and producers pay attention to indie authors who show they can sell. Because success talks. If you can prove your concept (and come with a built-in audience), you've got negotiating power.

One standout example? Freida McFadden, a powerhouse indie author who turned smart publishing choices into a blockbuster career.

CASE STUDY: FREIDA MCFADDEN

The Indie Power Move That Took Her from Kindle to Lionsgate

Freida McFadden began her writing career by self-publishing her first book, *The Devil Wears Scrubs*, on Amazon in 2013. As a practicing physician specializing in brain injury, she drew upon her medical background to craft compelling narratives.

Over the years, McFadden consistently released psychological thrillers, many of which gained traction through Kindle Unlimited and word-of-mouth recommendations. Her breakthrough came with *The Housemaid* (2022), an international bestseller that sold over 3.6 million English-language copies and held a long-running position on both *The New York Times* and Amazon bestseller lists. Its popularity led to a Lionsgate film adaptation directed by Paul Feig and starring Sydney Sweeney and Amanda Seyfried.

McFadden's journey from self-publishing to mainstream success exemplifies how indie authors can leverage their work to achieve broader opportunities without sacrificing creative control.

So Why Doesn't Everyone Go Indie?

Because it's hard.

There's no sugarcoating it: self-publishing is work. You'll need to make decisions, spend money, manage professionals, and market your book. You'll also make mistakes and (hopefully) learn from them.

You have to have the motivation and the perseverance to

tackle every part of publishing every day. This only works for those who are self-starters.

But here's the upside: you own everything. The ISBN. The files. The royalties. The brand.

Indie authors aren't publishing renegades. They're entrepreneurs with a plan. And the best ones treat their publishing journey like the business it is.

Yes, There's a Learning Curve, But You've Got This

Self-publishing is a skill set. You're not expected to know everything from day one. But every part of it—from cover design to metadata to marketing—is learnable. And I will walk you through each of them in the coming chapters.

And, now that you know the road you're taking, it's time to talk about the engine that drives everything: your book. Specifically, how to write a book that readers actually want to buy.

Let's dig into what it really means to write what sells ... without selling out.

CHAPTER 3

Write What Sells (Without Selling Out)

"Writing for the market" does not mean chasing trends or abandoning your voice. It means understanding the expectations of your genre and audience, then delivering a book that feels both fresh and familiar.

Think about your favorite authors. They don't reinvent the wheel with every book. They build trust. They create a brand. And they deliver on the promise their genre implies. You never finish a thriller by David Baldacci and wonder if it was secretly a romantic comedy halfway through. You know what you're getting—and that's why you buy it.

Writing to market means:

- Knowing the conventions of your genre (and when to break them)

- Understanding reader desires and emotional payoffs

- Crafting a reading experience that aligns with expectations ... then exceeds them

It doesn't mean being formulaic (although that sometimes works). It means being intentional. And when you're intentional, you're in control of how your book is received.

The key is to find the overlap between what you love to write and what your audience wants to read. That's the sweet spot where passion meets purpose—and where books sell.

If you are committed to being an indie publisher, you must learn what the market desires from their books. (And provide it.)

To learn more about writing to market, let's turn to Chris Fox, the guy who literally wrote the book on it.

CASE STUDY: CHRIS FOX

Writing to Market Without Selling Out

When indie author Chris Fox set out to make writing his full-time career, he didn't leave his success to chance. He approached publishing like a business with strategy, research, and intentional product-market fit. The result? A scalable writing career built on giving readers exactly what they wanted.

While the concept of writing to market existed long before him (as Fox himself has noted) he is widely credited with popularizing the term and practice in the indie publishing world through his bestselling book *Write to Market: Deliver a Book That Sells* (2016). In it, he dismantles the myth that writing to market means "selling out" or compromising creativity. Instead, he reframes it as writing with strategy: understanding reader expectations, identifying underserved niches, and crafting stories that both excite the author and appeal to a hungry audience.

His breakout *Destroyer* series was the product of this approach. Fox analyzed trends in science fiction, identified popular tropes (like alien invasions, reluctant heroes, and military action), and released the first book quickly—perfectly positioned for genre fans. It hit the charts and launched a full series.

Key takeaways from Chris Fox's success:

- He didn't guess. He researched. He studied what was selling, why it was working, and how he could bring something fresh to a proven formula.

- He leaned into genre expectations. Rather than trying to reinvent the wheel, he delivered exactly what readers were looking for—better and faster.

- He launched fast. Using a rapid release strategy, he maximized momentum and visibility in Amazon's algorithm.

- He treated writing like a business. He wrote what he loved, but he didn't ignore the market. He merged passion with practicality.

Fox's message isn't just for sci-fi writers. It's a universal truth for indie authors: If you want your books to sell, you need to write something people want to read and package it like a product designed for them.

Concept and Hook: Your First Strategic Choice

Before you write a word, your concept needs to work. That means:

- Is this a story or book idea with clear appeal?
- Can it be explained in one or two compelling sentences?
- Is there a built-in market for this kind of content?

A strong hook isn't about marketing, it's about clarity. It's the promise your book makes to the reader. Break that promise, and you lose trust. Nail it, and you gain loyalty.

First Impressions Are Everything

Readers give you maybe a page or two to prove your book is worth their time. If your opening doesn't grip them, you're done.

That's why your first chapter needs to:

- Introduce a compelling character or problem.

- Create tension, curiosity, or emotional resonance.

- Establish your tone and voice right away.

- For non-fiction, it is important to immediately show the reader that you understand and can solve their problem.

You don't need explosions or dead bodies in the first paragraph (unless you're writing thrillers, in which case maybe you do). But you do need forward momentum and emotional investment. Fast.

Understanding Reader Psychology

Readers don't buy books because they owe you something. They buy books because they want a specific emotional experience or outcome.

For fiction:

- **Excitement:** action, high stakes, fast pacing

- **Escape:** immersive world, strong characters, emotional stakes

- **Curiosity:** mystery, puzzles, clever twists
- **Inspiration:** growth arcs, wisdom, relatability
- **Comfort:** predictable structure, familiar tropes, hopeful resolutions

For nonfiction:

- **Clarity:** answers to a specific question or problem
- **Confidence:** tools or knowledge to take action
- **Relief:** a way out of confusion, pain, or overwhelm
- **Empowerment:** a sense of control or momentum
- **Connection:** a voice that understands and reflects their experience

When you know what your reader wants to feel or achieve, you can write with purpose, and that is what turns a good book into one that sparks sales and loyalty.

Writing to market starts with mindset but it only works when you deeply understand the readers you're writing for. That's where genre mastery comes in. In the next chapter, we'll explore how to position your book so it meets (and exceeds) reader expectations—without becoming formulaic or forgettable.

CHAPTER 4

Genre Is a Promise, Make Sure You Keep It

Now that you're thinking strategically about writing what sells, it's time to sharpen your focus on the lens through which readers discover your book: *genre*. Genre is more than a label; it's a contract. And if you break it, readers won't forgive you.

Know Your Genre Inside and Out

If you can't clearly define your book's genre, your readers won't be able to either—and that's a problem. Genres aren't boxes to confine you. They're bridges to your readers. They tell browsers what kind of story or value they're going to get.

Your job is to:

- Read 10–20 bestselling books in your target genre.

- Analyze what readers love *and* what they complain about.

- For fiction, take notes on tropes, pacing, structure, tone, and character arcs.

- With nonfiction, pay close attention to what reviewers highlight as most helpful; those insights reveal what your audience values the most.

Don't skip this step. You wouldn't build a house without a blueprint. Don't write a book without understanding the architecture of the genre it lives in.

Who Are You Writing For?

Every successful product is created with the end user in mind. Your book is no different. Your reader is not a vague concept; they are a real person with real expectations, tastes, and emotional triggers.

Ask yourself:

- Who am I writing this for?
- What do they crave from a book?
- What sort of journey do I want to take them on?

Give your ideal reader a name. A background. A bookshelf. Know what else they read, what they love, what they hate. The more clearly you define them, the easier it becomes to write something they can't put down.

You can start the process of discovering your readers by investigating the fan bases of authors who write books similar to yours. People love talking about their favorite books online, and platforms like Reddit, Goodreads, and Facebook are all good places to find data about your potential readers.

Deliver the Promise of Your Premise

Before you can deliver on your book's promise, you need to know exactly what your readers are expecting because every genre comes with built-in assumptions. These expectations aren't limitations; they're signals. When readers pick up a romance, a thriller, or a memoir, they're looking for a specific kind of emotional or narrative experience. If you understand those expectations and meet them well, you earn trust and loyal fans.

Use this chart as a quick-reference guide to major genres and the promises they make to readers.

Major Category Genre Expectations

Genre	Reader Expectations
Romance	Central love story, emotional arc, satisfying ending (usually Happily Ever After or Happy For Now), chemistry, character growth
Mystery	A clear crime or puzzle to solve, clues and red herrings, logical resolution, satisfying reveal
Thriller/Suspense	High stakes, fast pacing, danger or tension throughout, twists, a compelling hero vs. villain dynamic
Fantasy	Immersive world-building, consistent magic systems or rules, epic stakes, clear protagonist journey
Science Fiction	Futuristic or speculative elements, technology or scientific innovation, social commentary or big ideas
Historical Fiction	Accurate time period details, historical context, character-driven plot grounded in real events or cultures

Horror	Sense of dread or fear, supernatural or psychological elements, clear threat, dark or unsettling payoff
Adventure	Quest or journey, external conflict, action-driven plot, hero facing escalating challenges
Young Adult (YA)	Teen protagonists, coming-of-age themes, fast pacing, emotional growth, high relatability
Middle Grade (MG)	Age-appropriate language and themes, friendship and growth, humor, adventure or mystery elements
Memoir	Personal truth, emotional honesty, relatable themes, strong narrative voice, cohesive arc
Self-Help	Clear problem and promised result, practical steps or advice, encouraging tone, credibility
Business/ Entrepreneurship	Actionable strategies, case studies or examples, credibility, focus on results or ROI
True Crime	Factual accuracy, investigative tone, timeline of events, insight into crime, victim sensitivity
Inspirational/ Spiritual	Uplifting or reflective tone, personal transformation, universal truths or faith-based perspective

Understanding these expectations is only the first step. The real challenge (and opportunity) is following through on what you've promised.

And whatever you promise in your blurb or first few pages you *must* deliver. If you pitch a mystery, resolve it. If you hint at a romance, give readers a satisfying emotional arc. If you claim you'll teach the reader how to do their taxes, make sure they walk away knowing how to do exactly that. This doesn't mean predictable. It means earned. Readers want the experience they were promised. If you bait and switch, they won't be back.

You're Not Just a Writer, You're a Brand

Your book isn't just a standalone product. It's a brand ambassador. Every page speaks to your future as an author.

- Is your voice consistent?
- Is your message or theme something you can build on?
- Is your writing recognizable across multiple books?

You don't have to know your entire brand at book one. But you do need to start thinking about what you want readers to associate with your name. Are you edgy? Wholesome? Smart? Sassy? Figure it out, then write to reinforce it.

CASE STUDY: WILLOW WINTERS

How She Built a Romance Brand, Not Just a Book

Willow Winters started writing in early 2016, shortly after the birth of her daughter. A voracious romance reader, she finally decided to turn her own story ideas into books and hasn't stopped since.

She didn't wait for a publisher to greenlight her vision. Willow self-published her first romance novel that year and quickly discovered what resonated most with readers. According to Willow, she writes by instinct and mood, creating books that range from sweet and swoony to dark and suspenseful. It was the darker stories that truly took off. By leaning into emotional, high-stakes romance with an addictive edge, she struck a chord with her audience and paid close attention to what they loved.

Winters built her brand not just on voice, but on consistency. She published prolifically, hooked readers with series, and developed a deep backlist that acted like a magnet for new fans. Her stories blended popular tropes—like enemies-to-lovers and alpha billionaires—with raw emotion, creating a style readers returned to again and again.

She didn't stop there. Through savvy use of Kindle Unlimited, she maximized visibility. With reader groups and newsletters, she kept fans engaged between releases. With audiobooks and translations, she expanded her global reach. Her strategy of delivering what readers crave but doing it her way is one indie authors would do well to study.

The takeaway here is that market-savvy isn't selling out. It's selling smart. Understand your genre, know your readers, and build a catalog that keeps them coming back.

Write With Intention, Not Just Inspiration

Yes, write to market. Yes, understand your genre. But don't lose your voice trying to be someone you're not. The magic happens when you marry your unique perspective with reader expectations.

The most successful indie authors write books that are personal and purposeful. Books that blend authenticity with structure. Passion with polish.

So go ahead and write the book of your heart. But make sure it's also the book your readers are looking for. And if you're not sure what that is yet? Time to do your research.

Writing for readers doesn't mean writing without heart. It means writing with intention. When you understand your genre, your audience, and your long-term strategy, your creativity gains direction. Because in this business, knowledge isn't just power—it's profit.

Mistakes That Kill Marketable Books

Before you hit publish, here's a checklist of common pitfalls that turn potential fans into one-star reviewers:

- Weak or confusing openings
- Flat or unrelatable characters (or, in nonfiction, lack of voice)
- Pacing issues
- Awkward dialogue or jargon-heavy prose
- Lack of editing
- Premises that don't deliver
- Factual inaccuracies
- Genre bait-and-switches
- Endings that fizzle
- Overpromising packaging (cover, title, blurb)

Now that you've learned how to understand your genre and write to your audience, it's time to define what success looks like to you, and how to align your publishing strategy to make it happen.

CHAPTER 5

What Does Success Look Like for You?

Before you spend a single dollar on editing or design, before you obsess over launch plans or ad spend, you need to answer one question:

What does success look like for you?

Not for your favorite author. Not for a Facebook group. Not for the algorithm. For you.

For many first-time authors, success equates to "instant bestseller." If that's your definition, it's time for a reality check. Your book will not be an instant bestseller. Want to know how I can say that so bluntly? Because there's no such thing. Even the books that look like they blew up overnight? They didn't.

Behind every so-called "overnight success" is months (or years) of writing, pitching, emailing, posting, ad-spending, list-building, and maybe even a little cosmic intervention. That person online claiming they hit #1 the day they uploaded their book? First off, what list? Amazon's category lists are miles away from a *New York Times* bestseller list. And even on smaller lists, we know better. Books don't take off by magic. There has to be an audience, and building that takes serious work behind the scenes before a book gains traction.

Busting the Bestseller Myth

Everyone wants their book to be a bestseller. It's understandable. Bestseller lists feel like validation. But let's unpack what that really means.

Which list? Amazon category? *New York Times*? *USA Today*? Because they're not the same.

Hitting an Amazon subcategory #1 spot might take a few dozen sales in an hour. That's not nothing, but it's not career-defining either.

The *New York Times* list? That requires thousands of sales in a single week, across multiple retailers, with a mix of print and digital, often backed by a traditional publisher's campaign and a touch of editorial magic (yes, the list is curated).

And even if you hit a bestseller list ... then what?

Success is not about a list. It's about building a career, growing an audience, and getting your book into the right hands, over time.

Bestseller Lists: The Inside Scoop

What does it look like behind the scenes of a bestseller campaign? Well, that depends.

All the bestseller lists have varied nuances and rules. Amazon updates their category bestseller lists daily. With over 10,000 book-specific categories available, that translates into thousands of chances for your book to become a bestseller each day.

USA Today, on the other hand, calculates sales from Monday through Sunday and publishes their bestseller lists consisting of the 150 top-selling titles each Wednesday.

The New York Times bases their weekly bestseller lists on "popular books in the United States," which allows for a certain amount of curation to determine the titles for each of their seven bestseller lists.

As one might imagine, the strategy used to make each bestseller list mentioned above will be drastically different based on the individual list requirements.

An Amazon category bestseller campaign usually consists of researching niche categories to place a book in and pushing sales with ads or a discount eBook promotion over the course of a day or two. Depending on the category your title is competing in, a book can make #1 bestseller on Amazon with as few as three book sales.

USA Today counts pre-order sales on the day of release, making a pre-order campaign many authors' best chance of making the list. For books that have already been released, authors rely heavily on snagging a BookBub Featured Deal, which can result in upwards of 2,000 sales. Either strategy, when paired with additional eBook discount newsletters and advertising on social media, Amazon, BookBub, and Goodreads, gives authors a decent shot of making the 3,000–5,000 sales typically required to make the bestseller list. It's important to note, however, that *USA Today* requires that at least 500 of the weekly sales come from platforms other than Amazon.

The *New York Times* bestseller list is a harder nut to crack. While sales do play a part in becoming a *NYT* bestselling author (you will need 10,000–20,000 sales to make the list), the rules beyond that are murky. For example, bulk sales are included but only at the *Times'* discretion. And, aside from the sales requirement, the list is based on unpublished criteria that make a book "popular." It is rumored that the *Times* will review trending social media, news sites, blogs, podcasts, and magazines to determine a book's popularity.

Because of this, a *New York Times* bestseller campaign will often include heavy sales promotion in addition to a full PR campaign. The average *New York Times* bestseller campaign is alleged to cost in the range of five hundred thousand to one million dollars. Even a well-planned and well-funded campaign needs another secret ingredient that is rarely discussed: luck.

No marketing campaign—or budget—can guarantee a book will make it on a bestseller list. Planning, optimization, and marketing are important to the success of any bestseller campaign, but, even if you do everything right, a bestseller is never guaranteed.

Which is why an author should set both their expectations and their definition of success appropriately.

Hitting bestseller status is validating as an author, but it isn't the only measure of success. Becoming a published author, having readers who love your book, growing a dedicated following, and consistent sales are all valid measures of success. Make sure you celebrate each of them in turn.

The Reality Behind Book Sales

Need some perspective? Here are a few sobering (but important) stats from Circana BookScan, which tracks around 85% of US print book sales:

- Each year, fewer than 20 titles sell over a million copies across all formats, including print and eBooks. If we narrow that to just print books, the number drops by half.

- Less than 1% of books published in the last year sold over 500 copies.

- Major celebrities with big publisher backing, full PR tours, and talk show appearances sometimes sell just a few thousand copies.

- Over 80% of books, regardless of how they're published, lose money.

This isn't meant to discourage you. It's meant to inform you. Remember, knowledge is power. And the more realistic your goals, the better able you will be to achieve those goals.

Now the big question. What does it take to sell 1,000 copies, 5,000 copies, 100,000 copies? A plan, a budget, thick skin, impeccable timing, relentless hustle—and yes, a little luck.

Many well-written, highly marketable books barely crack a few hundred sales. Meanwhile, some offbeat, typo-ridden titles inexplicably rise far beyond their publisher's expectations. There's an undeniable randomness when a book captures the public's imagination.

As much as we in the industry would like to think we have the magic formula worked out, we are as clueless as the rest when a book races to the top of the charts. There's no proven formula for a bestseller. But there are foundational strategies that set successful books apart. And that's exactly what we're going to cover next.

Defining Your Version of Success

So let's ask it again. What does success look like for you?

- Is it holding your finished book in your hands?
- Is it seeing your book reviewed by strangers?
- Is it being invited to speak at conferences?
- Is it building a business around your writing?
- Is it helping people learn, laugh, or heal?

Every goal is valid—as long as it's yours. Take a moment to write it down. Not the dream someone sold you. The one you actually want.

Turning Your Definition Into a Strategy

Once you've defined your version of success, ask yourself:

- What kind of book will help me get there?
- Who needs to read it?
- What format, timeline, or platform supports that goal?

These answers become the filter you'll use in every decision that follows: budgeting, cover design, marketing, even how you show up online.

When you know what you're aiming for, it's easier to:

- Create a timeline.
- Set a budget.

- Choose the right publishing path.

- Say "no" to distractions.

Because without a target, you'll chase every trend, buy every course, and still feel like you're behind.

Playing the Long Game

Publishing is not a one-book business. Most successful authors don't hit their stride until their third, fourth, or fifth title.

If you're in this for the long haul, then early metrics don't define you, they inform you.

Every launch teaches you something. Every reader connection adds to your platform. Every review (even the bad ones) helps shape your future books.

The key is consistency, not instant fame.

So take the pressure off. You're not falling behind; you're building something one smart, strategic step at a time.

CHAPTER 6

What It Really Takes to Win in Self-Publishing

Self-publishing success is not about talent alone. It's about approach. About mindset. About treating your writing career like the business it is.

Too many indie authors hold themselves back, not because their books aren't good, but because their mindset is stuck in hobby mode. If you want to level up, you have to stop thinking like "just a writer" and start thinking like a professional.

That starts with understanding this fundamental truth:

Your Book Is a Product

It may be deeply personal. It may be your art, your heart, your story. But once it's published? It's also a product. And products need packaging, positioning, pricing, distribution, and marketing.

This doesn't mean you stop caring about your book. It means you care enough to give it a fighting chance in the market.

You Are the Publisher

Whatever your reason for self-publishing may be—just make sure it's a good one—you are going to be a published author and, by extension, a publisher.

You choose:

- How to price your book
- Which distributors to use
- How to format and package the product
- Where and how to market it

That's a lot of responsibility. But it also means you have the power to shape your career. Owning that role is what separates successful indies from those still spinning their wheels.

The Investment Triangle

Successful self-publishing is built on three core investments:

- **Time:** to write, revise, market, and learn.
- **Money:** to hire professionals, build assets, and run ads.
- **Energy:** the sustainable drive to show up consistently.

Most authors can afford two. Few can afford all three. But knowing your strengths and gaps lets you build a plan that works *for you.*

If you're not budgeting, you're gambling

This sample publishing budget can be customized for your goals, genre and distribution strategy. It might also be impacted by your own personal skills or those you're willing to learn to decrease costs. It is based on an 80,000 word manuscript.

Sample Indie Author Publishing Budget

Line Item	Low Estimate	High Estimate
Editing		
Developmental Editing	$1,000	$6,500
Line Editing	$800	$3,000
Copyediting	$600	$1,600
Proofreading	$400	$800
Design & Formatting		
Cover Design (eBook + Print)	$300	$1,200
Interior Formatting	$0	$800
ISBNs (Bowker in US)	$125	$295+
Barcodes	$0	$50
Publishing & Distribution		
IngramSpark Setup	$0	$99
Proof Copies (test run)	$20	$100
Return Reserve	$100	$500+
Marketing & Launch		
ARC Distribution, Email Tools	$50	$1250
Paid Ads	$200	$5,000+
BookBub Featured Deal (if lucky)	$200	$2,000+
Marketing / VA Support	$300	$3,000+
Author Platform & Tools		
Website (domain + hosting)	$100	$500+
Email Marketing Platform	$0	$3000/year
Canva Pro / Design Tools	$0	$120/year
Total Estimate	~$4,000	$28,000+

Always build in a 10–20% buffer for surprise costs, shipping, rush jobs, or marketing pivots.

Data Over Drama

Professionals don't panic over every one-star review. They don't make business decisions based on Facebook group gossip. They look at the data:

- What's my sell-through rate from Book 1 to Book 2?
- Which keywords are converting on Amazon?
- Where are my readers coming from and can I contact them directly?
- What ad creatives are delivering the best ROI?

This doesn't mean you become a robot. It means you make informed decisions. Feelings matter but facts win the long game.

Consistency Over Hustle

Indie authors often burn out trying to "do everything." That's not sustainable, and it's not professional.

Pros build systems to conserve their energy. They plan. They batch. They automate. They show up consistently, not chaotically.

A consistent author:

- Sends a regular newsletter
- Publishes on a reliable schedule
- Shows up in one or two key marketing channels

You don't need to hustle 24/7. You need a repeatable system you can sustain.

Confidence Without Ego

Being a pro doesn't mean pretending to know everything. It means being willing to learn. To hire experts. To revise. To improve.

Your first book won't be perfect. Your first launch might flop. Your first ads might burn money.

That's okay. Every pro was once a beginner who kept going.

The indie mindset is about embracing both the freedom and the responsibility of your publishing journey.

You don't have to do everything yourself. But you do have to lead the team you put together.

The Hobbyist vs. the Entrepreneur

The moment you decide to publish a book, you face a choice: will you be a hobbyist, or will you be an entrepreneur?

There's no shame in writing as a hobby. If your goal is to create something personal, share it with family, or check "write a book" off your bucket list, that's completely valid.

But if you want to sell books—if you want to earn money, build a platform, or grow an author career—you need to operate like an entrepreneur.

What's the Difference?

The Hobbyist Mindset:

- Writes when inspiration strikes
- Publishes to "see what happens"
- Avoids marketing because it feels uncomfortable
- Tries to do everything themselves to save money
- Reacts emotionally to reviews and sales numbers

The Entrepreneur Mindset:

- Sets goals and builds a plan
- Treats publishing as a business
- Learns marketing as a skill, not a burden
- Builds a team of professionals
- Makes decisions based on data and strategy

Entrepreneurs don't always get it right on the first try but they learn from their mistakes and try again. They test, adjust, and move forward with purpose.

Why It Matters

Your mindset determines your outcomes.

Hobbyists wait to feel ready. Entrepreneurs take the next step, even if they're scared.

Hobbyists hope people will find their book. Entrepreneurs build paths that lead readers right to it.

Hobbyists get stuck. Entrepreneurs grow.

You don't need to go full-time to think like an entrepreneur. You just need to commit to your career the way you've committed to your craft.

The Author Business Checklist

Want to know if you're acting like an author-entrepreneur? See how many of these you can check off:

- You have a professional author website.
- You've set up an email list (and send newsletters regularly).

- You are connecting with readers and fans of your genre online daily.

- You know your ideal reader (and where to reach them).

- You track your book sales, ad spend, and ROI.

- You're building a backlist, not banking on one book.

If you're not there yet, that's okay. The point isn't to shame you, it's to show you what's possible when you shift from dabbling to building.

Because the truth is, hobbyists burn out. Entrepreneurs build momentum.

CASE STUDY: CRAIG MARTELLE

From Indie Author to Publishing Powerhouse

If you're wondering what it looks like to fully embrace the entrepreneur mindset in indie publishing, look no further than Craig Martelle.

A retired Marine turned prolific author, Martelle didn't just dip his toe into self-publishing. He cannonballed in. He built a thriving career by writing fast, publishing often, and treating his author business with the discipline and systems of a military operation.

Martelle found early success writing military science fiction that delivered exactly what genre fans craved: action, pacing, and polish. But it wasn't just the writing that drove his rise; it was the strategy behind it. He built a wide backlist, released consistently, and optimized every piece of the publishing process for long-term growth. Like a true entrepreneur, he made data-driven decisions, tested what worked, and reinvested in his business.

But Martelle didn't stop with personal success. In 2015, he partnered with author Michael Anderle to help manage and grow the now-legendary 20BooksTo50K® Facebook group. The name came from a simple but powerful concept: if one well-marketed book could earn $7 a day, then 20 could generate a $50,000 annual income. That math—and the mindset behind it—ignited a global community. Under Martelle's stewardship, 20BooksTo50K® became one of the most influential support networks for indie authors, with tens of thousands of members sharing advice, resources, and success stories. What sets Martelle apart isn't just his output or income. It's his commitment to helping others succeed. Through conferences, workshops, and constant online engagement, he's turned his personal success into a rising tide for the entire indie publishing world.

Martelle's story proves that sustainable author careers aren't built on luck, hype, or hope. They're built on systems, consistency, and community. He didn't wait for the traditional publishing world. He made a plan, worked the plan, and brought thousands of authors along for the ride.

If you treat publishing like a hobby, it will pay you like a hobby. If you treat it like a business, you've got a real shot at building something successful, sustainable, and maybe even fun.

Take Yourself Seriously

When you treat yourself like a professional, others will too.

That means:

- Investing in quality editing and design

- Showing up consistently (not just at launch)

- Learning how to talk about your book without apologizing

- Planning for success and tracking your results

It means building an actual business around your books.

Whether that means a wide backlist, a connected platform, or offers beyond your book (like courses, speaking, or services), the goal is the same: sustainable income doing what you love.

Are You Ready to Dive In?

Publishing your book as an indie author can be thrilling, overwhelming, and deeply rewarding. You're choosing to take charge of your career, your creative vision, and your business.

But success doesn't happen by accident. It happens when authors go in with eyes wide open, do the work, and build their platform with strategy and intention.

So ask yourself:

- Am I ready to take ownership of my book's success?

- Am I prepared to make business-minded decisions?

- Am I willing to adapt when things don't go my way?

- Am I willing to learn what I don't know ... and pay for what I can't do?

- Am I in this for the long haul?

If the answer is yes—even if it's a nervous yes—then you're in the right place.

CHAPTER 7

How to Build Sustainable Success

Self-publishing success doesn't come from hustle alone. It comes from sustainability. Too many indie authors sprint through a book launch, only to burn out on the other side. What separates thriving indie authors from overwhelmed hobbyists isn't necessarily talent or budget; it's how they manage their time, energy, and expectations.

This chapter is about designing a professional rhythm that supports both your writing and your publishing responsibilities. It's about showing up consistently without crashing, and creating a work structure that helps you build momentum, avoid burnout, and keep your author career moving forward.

The Real Workload of an Indie Author

Indie authors wear a lot of hats. On any given week, you might be:

- Writing or revising your manuscript
- Communicating with editors or formatters

- Creating or approving design assets
- Managing publishing timelines and uploads
- Marketing your book (social media, email, ads, PR, outreach)
- Tracking finances, royalties, and business operations
- Building your platform (website, newsletter, community)

That's a lot and it's easy to feel like you're always behind. But the key to staying on track isn't doing more. It's doing the right things consistently.

Avoiding Burnout Through Systems and Boundaries

Indie authors often fall into two extremes: obsessive overcommitment or avoidance driven by overwhelm. Neither is sustainable.
Instead, build repeatable systems:

- **Themed days:** Assign broad focus areas to each day (e.g., Monday = Marketing, Tuesday = Writing, Friday = Admin).
- **Time blocks:** Use calendar blocks to dedicate specific hours to deep work vs. communication or content creation.
- **Batching tasks:** Write multiple blog posts or social media captions in one sitting. Schedule them in advance.
- **Digital boundaries:** Limit email or social media to set windows. Protect your creative time.

You are your most valuable asset. Your calendar should reflect that.

A Weekly Rhythm That Works for You

There's no such thing as a "one-size-fits-all" author schedule. Some indie authors write full-time. Others are squeezing in creativity between shifts, school pickups, or second jobs. Both are valid, and both can lead to publishing success.

The key is building a repeatable rhythm that matches your life, energy, and goals. That rhythm won't look the same for everyone, and that's exactly the point.

Let's look at two sample workflows to show how success can be built from *either* end of the time-availability spectrum.

Sample Weekly Workflow: Part-Time Author

If you're balancing a day job, caregiving, or other major responsibilities, your time is limited—but your progress doesn't have to be. The trick is consistency over volume.

This schedule is designed for someone with 30–60 minutes per day to dedicate to their writing business:

Day	Focus Area	Key Activities (30–60 minutes max)
Monday	Micro Marketing	Schedule 1–2 social posts, respond to reader messages, share a blog/article link.
Tuesday	Creative Work	Write or revise for 30 minutes. Use voice notes during commute or breaks.
Wednesday	Admin & Check-in	Review sales, check in with editors/designers, update metadata if needed.
Thursday	Platform Building	Draft newsletter or reply to reader emails. Do light engagement online.
Friday	Business Growth	Watch a webinar, update your budget, or learn a new marketing tactic.
Saturday	Deep Work	Carve out a longer writing block (1–2 hours). Use this time for creative focus.
Sunday	Planning & Reset	Reflect on the week, plan next week's top 3 goals, schedule key tasks.

If you only have 20 minutes, pick one "needle-mover" task: write 250 words, send one pitch, or schedule one social post. Progress adds up.

Sample Weekly Workflow: Full-Time Indie Author

If you're treating your publishing career as a full-time business, structure becomes even more essential. Without clear focus, time can slip through the cracks. This schedule builds in themed days to maintain momentum and prevent burnout:

Day	Focus Area	Key Activities
Monday	Marketing & Outreach	Schedule social posts, pitch podcasts, follow up on reviews.
Tuesday	Deep Writing	Draft or revise your current work in progress (WIP).
Wednesday	Production & Admin	Coordinate with editors/designers, update metadata, manage uploads.
Thursday	Platform & Community	Write newsletters, reply to reader emails, engage on social media.
Friday	Business & Learning	Analyze sales, update your budget, take a course, read industry blogs.
Saturday	Creative Expansion	Brainstorm new ideas, read widely, explore content formats like video or podcast.
Sunday	Light Touch / Rest	Plan the week ahead, do light updates, rest and reset.

This model isn't a rulebook. It's a framework. Feel free to tweak, reorder, or condense depending on your personal energy levels, deadlines, or creative flow. Just keep in mind: daily writing is assumed for full-time authors, even on theme days that don't call it out directly.

Whether you're part-time or full-time, the secret isn't having more hours, it's knowing how to use the ones you have with purpose.

The Power of Tiny Habits

Big launches and long marketing plans matter. But the engine of your career is built from smaller, daily commitments:

- Writing consistently

- Checking in on your goals

- Maintaining relationships with your team and readers

- Learning, adjusting, and iterating

You don't need to work 12-hour days. You just need to keep moving.

10–30 minutes of strategic effort per day can compound into real results over time. Whether that's writing 500 words, sending a pitch, learning a new tool, or scheduling a reader email, small steps are how real careers are built.

Example: 10-Minute Marketing Moments

At New Shelves, we often talk about "10-Minute Marketing Moments": bite-sized author tasks that fit easily into your day without hijacking your writing time. These might include updating your Goodreads profile, writing a social media caption, submitting your book for a review, or replying to a reader email. Each one may seem small on its own, but compounded daily over a year, they add up to over 60 hours of meaningful book marketing.

You don't need a complicated plan.
You need consistent action.

Your Creative Rhythm Is a Business Strategy

There's no single right way to schedule your author life. But here are a few principles that successful indie authors use:

- Treat writing time like a meeting. Show up. Don't cancel.

- Protect your peak creative hours. Don't waste your best brain on email.

- Audit your time monthly. What's working? What's draining you?

- Define your success metrics. Are you writing the books you want to write? Reaching the readers who matter?

Consistency isn't just a creative habit. It's a business decision. Your calendar, habits, and systems should support your long-term growth, not sabotage it.

Before we dive deeper into the production side of publishing (like editing, formatting, and design), take a moment to ask:

- What does your ideal work week look like?

- Where are you wasting time?

- What's one habit you could build this week to support your author goals?

The authors who thrive in this business aren't the ones with the flashiest launches. They're the ones who keep showing up week after week with purpose and persistence.

Let's keep the momentum going. Next up: Creating a book that sells, and the team of pros you'll need to make it happen.

PART II

Creating a Book That Sells

CHAPTER 8

Finding Your Dream Team

One of the biggest myths in indie publishing is that you can (or should) do everything yourself. Yes, you are the publisher. But just like any successful publisher, your job is to assemble a team of professionals who will elevate your manuscript from a draft to a commercially competitive book.

This chapter is about making the right hires, asking the right questions, and avoiding the costly mistakes that too often trip up even the most talented authors.

Deciding What to Own vs. Delegate

Before you start hiring, take a moment to decide where your time, skills, and energy are best spent.

Ask yourself:

- Do I have professional-level skills in this area?

- Do I have the time to learn and execute it at a high standard?

- Will DIYing this aspect improve the final product ... or compromise it?

Your role is to be the creative visionary and the decision-maker, not the formatter, typesetter, or emergency file fixer at midnight the week of launch.

Focus on what only you can do: writing a great book and making high-level publishing decisions. Then bring in professionals to handle the rest.

Some tasks are relatively safe to DIY—like eBook formatting with tools like Vellum or Atticus—if you're comfortable with tech. Others, like cover design and developmental editing, are high-risk to do alone.

Who You'll Need on Your Team

The makeup of your team will depend on your book, budget, and goals, but here's a core lineup most indie authors rely on:

- **Developmental Editor:** Helps shape the structure and substance of your book

- **Copyeditor:** Polishes grammar, clarity, and readability

- **Proofreader:** Catches typos, formatting issues, and layout mistakes post-typesetting

- **Cover Designer:** Creates your book's most important marketing tool

- **Interior Designer/Formatter:** Ensures your book looks professional on every page

- **Marketing/PR Support:** Assists with launch strategy, ads, and outreach

Where to Find Professionals You Can Trust

Start with books you admire. Flip to the acknowledgments or copyright page and see who the author worked with. You can also search their name on LinkedIn or ask your author network for contact info.

There are excellent professional directories and author organizations that can help you find vetted service providers including the Alliance of Independent Authors (ALLi), Independent Book Publishers Association (IBPA), Editorial Freelance Association (EFA), Reedsy, and more, as seen in the table below.

Resource	Description
Independent Book Publishers Association (ibpa-online.org)	Education, advocacy, and a vetted service provider directory
Alliance of Independent Authors (ALLi) (allianceindependentauthors.org)	Author support, industry watchdog reports, and trusted partner directory
Authors Guild (authorsguild.org)	Legal resources, contract review, and career support for published authors
Reedsy (reedsy.com)	Curated marketplace for professional editors, designers, marketers, and formatters
Editorial Freelancers Association (the-efa.org)	Trusted source for freelance editors and proofreaders

Resource	Description
New Shelves Books (newshelves.com)	Marketing, distribution, and retail support for authors
Creative Hotlist (creativehotlist.com)	Portfolio-based directory of designers and publishing creatives
99designs (99designs.com)	Global design marketplace, including book covers and author branding
Behance (behance.net)	Showcase of top creative professionals, including book designers
MediaBistro (mediabistro.com)	Freelance talent for publishing, PR, and production
ACES: The Society for Editing (aceseditors.org)	Professional editing standards and searchable member directory
Upwork / Fiverr Pro (upwork.com / fiverr.com)	General freelance platforms (use caution: vet credentials and publishing experience carefully)

Ask Better Questions

Before hiring anyone, ask:

- Could you share an example of a recently published book you've worked on in my genre?

- What does your process and communication style look like?

- What's your average turnaround time?

- Can I contact 2–3 of your current and past clients for references?

- Do you work under a written agreement with deliverables?

How to Evaluate Their Answers

- **Published Samples:** Are the books well-reviewed and genre-appropriate?

- **Communication:** Are they prompt, professional, and clear in your early exchanges?

- **References:** Contact references and ask, "Would you hire this person again?" and "What challenges, if any, came up?"

- **Rates:** If pricing seems too low, ask what's included ... and what's not. Clarity matters more than cost.

Still torn between two qualified options? Ask for a paid sample. Most editors will review 1,000 words for a small fee. Designers can often provide a rough concept. It's worth the investment.

Red Flags and Common Scams

There are incredible professionals in the publishing world, and there are predators. Watch out for:

- Publishing packages that retain your rights or royalties unless you're working with a verified hybrid publisher
- Services with no verifiable portfolio or references
- One-size-fits-all packages at bargain-bin prices
- Vague timelines and no written contract

Trust your instincts. If someone pressures you, dodges questions, or sounds too slick to be true, walk away.

Hiring Freelancers vs. Full-Service Teams vs. Hybrid Publishers

There are three main approaches to assembling your team:

Path	You Manage	Cost	Rights	Best For…
Freelancers	Yes	Low–Medium	Yours	Authors who want control
Full-Service Team	No	Medium–High	Yours	Authors who want ease and guidance
Hybrid Publisher	No	High	Shared	Authors seeking a partner approach

Freelancers give you maximum control and often lower costs, but you'll be managing all the moving parts yourself. Full-service teams offer a smoother ride, with built-in project management that can save time and stress. Hybrid publishers, as we've already discussed, operate more like traditional publishers. They may offer branding, design, and distribution services—but they typically retain the ISBN, influence product decisions, and take a share of your royalties.

If you're considering a hybrid publisher, vet them thoroughly. Request sample contracts, read reviews, and ask clear, concise questions. A reputable hybrid makes money from selling books, not just from selling dreams to authors. If most of their revenue comes from author fees rather than book sales, that's a red flag. In other words: make sure you're working with a professional partner, not a vanity press in disguise.

Protect Yourself and Your Project

Before anyone starts work:

- Get a written contract or agreement.
- Clarify payment terms, revision rounds, and delivery milestones.
- Ask for samples in your genre.
- Check at least two references.
- Use a 24-hour cooling-off period before committing.

Every agreement you enter is a professional transaction, and protecting yourself protects your book. Approach contracts, payments, and timelines with the same seriousness you'd bring to any other business investment—because that's exactly what this is.

How to Manage Your Team Without Micromanaging

Hiring a great team is only half the equation. Here's how to manage them effectively:

- Use simple tools to track progress: Google Docs, Trello, or a shared spreadsheet work well.

- Schedule weekly or milestone check-ins. Don't wait until the final deadline.

- Provide clear direction upfront (especially for design projects).

- Communicate early if something feels off.

- Respect their time, and ask them to respect yours.

The most successful indie authors aren't lone wolves. They're creative CEOs who build trusted teams.

In the next chapter, I will walk you through how to work effectively with your editor, formatter, and designer to bring your vision to life.

For now, remember: Your book deserves a professional team. Build one that matches your goals—and your standards. And once you've built your dream team, your next challenge is staying sane while using it.

CHAPTER 9

Editing Like a Publisher

Editing is where your draft becomes a book. It's the difference between a story that sort of works and one that hits all the right notes. And yes, it's the one step most self-published authors try to skip or skimp on ... which is a big reason why so many indie books fall flat.

Let's not do that.

If you want your book to compete in a professional marketplace, it needs to be professionally edited. That means hiring someone with industry experience—not your cousin Susie who teaches high school English. A professional editor will help shape your book from a content, structure, and clarity standpoint, ensuring it's the best version of itself before it ever hits the shelves.

You cannot edit your book yourself. You can *revise* your book, but editing a book is a professional's job. Doctors do not treat themselves or family members. This is a hard and fast rule.

> *Repeat Amy Collin's favorite phrase after me: You cannot lick your own elbow, and you cannot edit your own book.*

All Great Writers Have Editors

One of the biggest challenges new authors face is the isolation that comes with the creative process. Unlike painting or sculpting, writing—and especially publishing—cannot be done well in a vacuum. A written book is only half finished. It's the publisher's role to take the raw manuscript across the finish line, and that starts with building a strong team of industry professionals, beginning with a qualified editor.

Hiring a talented editor is just the first step. The real challenge is trusting them to do their job. It's one thing to hand over your manuscript, but it's another to accept honest feedback, suggested revisions, and the kind of tough love that turns good books into great ones. Find an editor you trust and respect, then let them do what you hired them to do.

Successful indie authors learn to separate their roles. Once the writer has finished, the publisher steps in. That shift in mindset—from creator to entrepreneur—is critical to self-publishing success.

The Editing Funnel

The editing process works best in stages. My good friend, Ericka McIntyre, explains the process of editing as a funnel: wide at the top, narrow at the bottom. As you move through the funnel, your book goes from big-picture restructuring to fine-detail polishing.

1. Developmental Editing: The Big, High-Level Edit

This is your "big picture" pass. A bird's eye view of your manuscript. A good developmental editor will ask:

- Does the narrative develop logically?
- Are there holes in the plot?
- Do character arcs make sense?
- Is something missing that readers will expect?
- For nonfiction: Are the arguments coherent and the structure logical?

2. Line Editing: Sentence-Level Clarity and Style

Line editors examine your manuscript line by line, polishing your prose for maximum clarity and impact. They evaluate:

- Sentence structure
- Word choice
- Voice and tone
- Flow and rhythm

This is where your manuscript gains sophistication and polish.

3. Copyediting: Grammar and Consistency

A copy editor checks for:

- Spelling and grammar
- Punctuation and syntax
- Style consistency
- Continuity and factual accuracy

They ensure consistency across chapters and spot small errors you're too close to see.

4. Proofreading: The Final Pass

Proofreaders review the formatted book and catch lingering issues:

- Typos and missing words
- Layout and spacing errors
- Header and footer inconsistencies
- Awkward line breaks and formatting glitches

Your proofreader is your last quality inspection before the book goes to print.

What Type of Editing Do You Need?

Every book can benefit from all four stages of editing. But depending on your strengths, you may need heavier support in one area than another. Here's a guide:

- If your plot is shaky or your structure feels off: Start with developmental editing.
- If your draft is clean but flat: Line editing can elevate it.
- If you're nearly done but not quite polished: Copyediting and proofreading are non-negotiable.

What Editors Don't *Do (Usually)*

Even the best editors won't:

- Format your book for print or eBook
- Write your product description or back cover copy
- Check every technical fact for accuracy

- Market your book

- Catch major plot or structure issues in the proofreading phase

Each editing stage has a distinct purpose. Make sure you're hiring the right person for the right phase, and setting the right expectations.

Editing Across Genres

Editing isn't one-size-fits-all. A romance novel needs emotional payoff and character chemistry. A business book needs clarity and a logical flow. A memoir needs pacing, reflection, and emotional resonance. Choose an editor who understands the unique expectations of your genre.

How to Find a Great Editor

Referrals from trusted author friends are often your best bet for finding a great editor. But if you're starting from scratch, you can also explore professional directories and vetted platforms such as the Editorial Freelancers Association (the-efa.org) or Reedsy, a marketplace of curated freelancers. Writing conferences and author groups are also excellent places to connect with experienced editors.

No matter where you find your candidates, always ask for a sample edit on your manuscript to evaluate fit. Review client testimonials or references, and clarify what the editor does and doesn't include in their services. Most importantly, make sure they understand your genre and your publishing goals. Editing literary fiction is very different from polishing a business book or prepping a cozy mystery.

What Does It Cost?

Professional editing should be seen as an investment in your book's success. And like any skilled professional, a good editor expects (and deserves) to be paid accordingly.

The Editorial Freelancers Association (EFA) publishes a detailed rate card breaking down editing costs across genres. According to the most recent chart averages, here's what you can expect to pay for a 60,000-word manuscript:

Editing Type	Cost per Word	Estimate for 60k Words
Developmental Editing	$0.03 -$0.08	$1,800 -$4,800
Line Editing	$0.02 -$0.05	$1,200 -$3,000
Copyediting	$0.01 -$0.03	$600 -$1,800
Proofreading	$0.005 -$0.01	$300 -$600

Yes, it adds up. But no, you shouldn't skimp. A well-edited book is more readable, more competitive, and far more likely to earn positive reviews and word-of-mouth sales.

Contracts and Communication

A professional editor will usually provide a written agreement outlining the scope of work, timelines, and payment terms. This document should spell out what's included (and not), the expected delivery dates, how revisions or follow-up questions are handled, and your payment schedule.

If the editor doesn't offer a contract, ask for one. Clear

agreements protect both parties and help avoid misunderstandings down the line.

Before You Hire an Editor

Before handing your manuscript to a professional editor, take the time to clean it up yourself. A thoughtful self-editing pass not only makes their job easier, but it can also reduce your editing bill significantly. Editors often charge more if they have to wade through careless or unpolished writing. Your goal is to give them the cleanest draft possible so they can focus on real improvements rather than avoidable sloppiness.

Start by setting the manuscript aside for a week or two. Coming back to it with fresh eyes will help you see what's actually on the page, not just what you *meant* to write. When you're ready to dive back in, read your book aloud. This will help you catch clunky sentences, awkward dialogue, or repeated phrases that your eyes might skip over. You should also run simple spelling and grammar checks through your word processor or a tool like Grammarly. It won't catch everything, but it will clean up the low-hanging fruit.

Next, look for common filler words that weaken your prose. Words like *just*, *very*, *really*, and *actually* often dilute your writing and can usually be cut without losing meaning. Another helpful strategy is to print out your manuscript or load it onto a tablet. Changing the reading format allows you to experience the book in a new way, helping you spot inconsistencies or pacing issues more easily.

Once your manuscript feels solid, consider enlisting early readers—specifically alpha and beta readers—before you move on to professional editing. Alpha readers are usually close to you (friends, critique partners, fellow writers) and read your manuscript early in the process. Their feedback tends to focus on big-picture issues like plot structure, character development, pacing, and tone. Think of alpha readers as your story's first round of diagnostics.

Beta readers, on the other hand, come in after you've already revised based on alpha feedback. Ideally, they resemble your target audience. These readers provide insight on the book's emotional impact, engagement level, and overall clarity. They're not looking to fix your plot holes; they're reacting to the reading experience.

While alpha readers can help shape your story during early drafts, beta readers offer a valuable perspective before final edits. Both are informal, unpaid roles, but the insights they offer are incredibly helpful, and they can save your editor from having to flag problems that could have been fixed earlier.

The cleaner and more thoughtfully revised your manuscript is before you hand it off, the more value you'll get from your professional editor. It's the difference between asking an editor to polish your work ... and expecting them to rescue it.

What About AI Editing Tools?

Tools like Grammarly, Hemingway, or ProWritingAid are useful but they are not editors. They can flag grammar mistakes, catch redundancies, and point out passive voice, but they can't understand story structure, nuance, or emotional resonance.

Use them early in your revision process, but don't rely on them for the final polish.

How to Accept Feedback Without Losing Your Mind

Getting an edit letter can feel like a gut punch. That's normal. But it's also a gift. Editors aren't trying to tear you down; they're trying to lift your book up.

Here's how to deal like a pro:

- Read the notes once. Then walk away.
- Let your ego cool. Then read them again.
- Take what resonates. Sit with what doesn't.
- Revise with purpose, not defensiveness.

> *Pros revise. Amateurs argue.*
> *You've got this.*

Editing Is Not Optional

You don't get a second chance at a first impression. If you want your book to compete with traditionally published titles, it has to *read* like one. That starts with editing—and ends with you publishing with confidence.

In the next chapter, we'll move into the visual side of publishing as we review the ins and outs of cover design. It's time to make your book irresistible at first glance.

CHAPTER 10

Cover Design That Sells

Your cover is not just a placeholder for your title. It is your book's first impression, its handshake, its elevator pitch. It's the split-second difference between "Ooh, what's this?" and a scroll-past you'll never recover from.

That old saying, *"Don't judge a book by its cover,"* might sound noble, but it doesn't hold up in publishing.

Readers judge. Reviewers judge. Retailers judge. We all do.

If you want to sell books, it's time to embrace that truth and back it up with a professional cover and a realistic design budget.

The Look of a Successful Book

Successful books look like other successful books. That doesn't mean your book has to be a clone, but it does mean it needs to follow the unspoken rules of its genre.

A cozy mystery with a horror aesthetic? Confusing. A steamy romance in sci-fi fonts and cold, metallic colors? Instant turn-off. Readers want to be reassured that your book will deliver the experience they're looking for, and that reassurance comes from your cover.

Your cover should align with genre conventions for:

- Font style and hierarchy
- Color palette and tone
- Image or illustration style
- Title and subtitle placement
- Author name treatment

Walk the aisles. Literally. Go to a bookstore, pick your category, and look around. What colors dominate? What kind of fonts are used? Which images stand out? Then go online and check out the top 20 bestsellers in your category. Create a swipe file or Pinterest board. Use it. Your cover should feel like it belongs with the books your audience is already buying.

What a Cover Designer Actually Does (and Why They're Worth It)

Hiring a professional cover designer is one of the best investments you can make. Great designers are visual marketers. They understand composition, genre cues, and how to make your book pop both in print and thumbnail form.

They're not just people who make things look nice. They're strategists. A great cover doesn't just attract any reader. It attracts the *right* reader. A professional cover whispers, "You want to read me."

General Pricing:

- Premade covers: $50–$200
- Custom eBook cover: $150–$400
- Full custom paperback: $300–$800
- Hardcover + dust jacket: $400–$1,200+

Finding the Right Designer

When hiring a designer, look for someone who specializes in book covers, has experience in your specific genre, and offers clear terms. This should include details like how many revision rounds are included, whether you'll receive the source files, and how image licensing is handled. Book your designer early as professionals with strong portfolios are often scheduled months in advance.

Your Role in the Process

Your designer isn't a mind reader. It's your job to come prepared. Before hiring, pull together a collection of book covers you love (and a few you dislike), identify your book's clear genre classification, and outline the emotional tone or mood you want the cover to convey. You should also define who your target audience is, including age, gender, and reading preferences if possible.

Once you've hired a designer, give them creative freedom but within a focused brief. Be involved in the process, but not overbearing. Set expectations early, ask for a couple of initial concept options, establish a realistic deadline, and keep communication clear and professional throughout.

DIY Cover Design? Tread Cautiously

If you choose to design your own book cover, know this: it must be indistinguishable from a professionally produced, traditionally published book. That's the standard. Anything less will signal "amateur" to readers, retailers, and reviewers, and it could cost you sales.

This is not a hurdle that can be overcome with gumption and style. This is not the place to try to DIY unless you have experience.

But if you are determined to design your own cover, avoid the most common mistakes. Skip the overused Canva templates. Stay away from generic fonts or clip art. And absolutely steer clear of anything with WordArt-style effects that announce your book as DIY rather than polished and professional.

If you're moving forward with designing it yourself, make sure to use the right tools and resources.

- **Layout tools** like Affinity Publisher and Adobe InDesign offer the precision needed for professional formatting.

- **Mockup platforms** such as BookBrush or Canva Pro can help you create early concepts, but they're not intended for final, print-ready files.

- **Image sources** like iStock, Deposit Photos, Unsplash, Pexels, and Pixabay offer licensed, high-quality visuals appropriate for commercial use.

- **Font libraries** such as Adobe Fonts and Google Fonts provide design-friendly typefaces that are safe and legible.

As you gather your assets, be cautious. Never use images

pulled from Pinterest or Google unless you have full commercial rights. Double-check licenses for all imagery. If you're using AI-generated art, verify that the source grants permission for commercial use. Some do not, and using them may get your book flagged by distributors or challenged by artists.

Unless you have formal design training and a clear understanding of print specifications—such as bleed, trim, DPI, and color profiles—it's still best to hire a professional designer.

> *A compelling, professionally executed cover is one of the most powerful sales tools you have. Don't let weak design hold your book back.*

What Makes a Cover Work?

- **Simple:** Not overcrowded with fonts or clutter
- **Genre-correct:** Matches reader expectations
- **Legible:** Title and author name readable at thumbnail size
- **Balanced:** Strong composition with visual flow

You're designing for:

- Print covers
- Thumbnails on retail sites
- Ads, social media, and email graphics

Title and Subtitle Strategy

Your title should be:

- Memorable
- Easy to say and spell
- Visually balanced in design

Your subtitle (especially for nonfiction) should:

- Clarify the book's benefit or message
- Use searchable language
- Support the promise of the book

Clarity trumps cleverness. Don't get too cute if it compromises understanding.

Series Branding Matters

If your book is part of a series, your covers should:

- Share consistent fonts, layout, and imagery style
- Be immediately recognizable as part of a set
- Reinforce a visual brand readers can return to

Series cohesion helps with binge-reading, shelf presence, and retailer promotions.

The Most Overlooked Part of Your Cover: The Spine

In brick-and-mortar stores, your spine is your cover. That tiny sliver of space is all most customers see.

Spine Design Tips:

- **Size:** Ensure your book is thick enough to support spine text (usually 100+ pages)
- **Color:** Analyze genre trends and stand out wisely
- **Text:** Large, bold, readable from a few feet away

Do the Bookstore Test:

Mock up your spine at full size, tape it to a shelf in your genre section, and step back. If it disappears, rethink your design.

Ask the Right Questions

Before finalizing your cover, ask:

- Who is this for?
- What promise does this book make?
- What's my one-line pitch?
- Do my comps accomplish what I want my book to do?
- Does this cover visually communicate genre?
- Can I read the title at thumbnail size?
- Would I pick this up in a store?

Your Cover Sells the Click

Especially in online retail, your cover is what entices a potential reader to click. If no one clicks, no one reads your blurb, sample chapter, or reviews.

A strong cover says: "This book is for you." And that's what gets it picked up, shared, and remembered.

What It All Comes Down To

Your book cover is not decoration. It's your top marketing asset. It needs to make the right promise to the right person at a glance. It needs to belong—and stand out—on the shelf or screen.

What your book looks like matters more than what it says, at least at first. That's not cynicism. That's strategy.

Next up: we bring the same professional polish to your interior, because what's inside needs to deliver on what your cover promises.

CHAPTER 11

Formatting: The Invisible Backbone of Your Book

Let's set the scene: your book has a killer title. The cover is on point. You've nailed your back cover copy and polished every sentence to a gleaming shine. Then someone opens the book ... and the text is crammed to the edges, the font screams "2003," and the chapter headings look like a PowerPoint slide.

Congratulations ... you've just lost the reader.

Formatting Isn't Just About Looking Good, It's About Reading Well

Formatting is the invisible backbone of book production. More than aesthetics, it's about functionality. When done well, it disappears and quietly powers readability, professionalism, and the reader's experience. When done poorly, it's impossible to ignore, making a book feel like it was printed at the office supply store and sticking out like Comic Sans in a legal brief.

What Is Formatting, Really?

Formatting is how your book is laid out on the page. It includes:

- Font choice and size
- Chapter headings and spacing
- Paragraph alignment and indents
- Margins and trim size
- Page numbers, headers, and footers
- Scene breaks and visual flow

Formatting is not just about making things "look pretty." It's about making your book easy (and enjoyable) to read. It's also about meeting the technical requirements of distribution platforms.

And if you're skipping this step? You're not self-publishing. You're self-sabotaging.

Print vs. eBook Formatting

Formatting for print and formatting for eBooks are completely different processes. Print books are static—each page is fixed and designed with precision. eBooks, on the other hand, are dynamic and reflowable, adjusting to the reader's screen size and settings.

Print Formatting Must-Haves:

Print formatting requires attention to physical layout and aesthetics. Be sure to include:

- Gutter margins for proper binding
- Classic, readable fonts such as Garamond, Minion Pro,

Georgia, or Baskerville

- Consistent styling for chapter titles and scene breaks
- Clean line breaks with widows and orphans avoided
- Page numbers placed appropriately (not on blank pages or chapter openers)

eBook Formatting Must-Haves:

Digital formatting is a different animal entirely. To ensure accessibility and a professional reading experience:

- Avoid tabs, spacebar indents, and hard returns
- Use a reflowable layout that adapts to different screen sizes and reader settings
- Apply logical heading styles to create built-in navigation
- Include a clickable table of contents
- Omit page numbers, as they're meaningless on digital devices

A Note on Fixed-Format eBooks:

Fixed-format eBooks are designed to preserve layout and image placement, and are typically used for:

- Children's picture books
- Cookbooks
- Art books or photography collections

That said, they come with notable drawbacks:

- Limited device compatibility
- Higher production costs

- Poor accessibility for many readers
- Restricted distribution options

Unless your book's value depends on exact visual layout, reflowable formatting is the preferred option for eBooks. It ensures broader accessibility, easier distribution, and a smoother experience for most readers.

Formatting Tools: DIY or Hire a Pro?

If you're tech-savvy and enjoy control, there are excellent DIY tools. But if your book includes images, charts, poetry, or tables, or if you just want peace of mind, hire a professional.

Quick Comparison: DIY Formatting Tools

Tool	Platform	Price (2025 est.)	Best For	Watch Out For
Vellum	Mac only	$199 (eBook) / $249 (Print + eBook)	Industry gold standard	Requires Mac
Atticus	Mac & PC	$147 (One-time)	Print + eBook, beginner friendly	Still adding features
Reedsy	Web-based	Free	Clean, basic layout	Limited customization
Scrivener	Mac & PC	~$59	Drafting + compiling	Not user-friendly for formatting

Tool	Platform	Price (2025 est.)	Best For	Watch Out For
Canva	Web-based	Free / $120/ yr (Pro)	Visual books (children's, art)	Bleed/ margin specs tricky
Word	PC & Mac	Free (if owned)	Emergency backup only	Formatting instability

Hiring a Professional Formatter

A good formatter knows:

- Bleed settings, gutter margins, and DPI

- How to create files that pass KDP and IngramSpark reviews

- What each platform requires to approve your uploads

General Rates:

- Simple eBook or Print: $150-500

- Complex Layouts (images, charts, etc.): $500-$2,500+

Ask before hiring:

- What file types will I get? (InDesign, ePub, PDF, etc.)

- Are source (design) files included in the price?

- How many revisions are included?

- Will you provide both eBook and print versions?

- Can I see a formatting sample before final delivery?

Amateur Mistakes

Readers might not always know *why* your book feels off, but they'll sense it. Common red flags include double spaces after periods, inconsistent paragraph spacing or indents, oversized or squint-worthy fonts, and missing headers or footers. Poor justification that leaves rivers of white space and margins with no breathing room can also make your book feel more like a Word document than a professionally published title. If that's the case, it's time for a redesign.

Accessibility and Readability

Formatting plays a crucial role in both the look and usability of your book. Accessibility matters—not just ethically, but strategically. Choose dyslexia-friendly fonts where possible, avoid full justification that disrupts flow, and ensure logical navigation and clickable elements in your eBook. Across all formats, use a minimum 11-point font with high contrast (such as black on white or cream) to support readability for all readers.

> *Accessible = more readable.*
> *More readable = more marketable.*

Platform Requirements: One File Does Not Fit All

Different platforms may require different specs for upload and printing.

Amazon KDP:

- File types: ePub (eBook), PDF (print), Word (.docx) (print and eBook)*

- Fonts must be embedded

- No bleed errors or placeholder text

* Word (.docx) files are accepted but not recommended for professional publishing.

IngramSpark:

- File types: ePub (eBook), PDF/X-1a (print)

- Embed fonts and follow their trim/bleed template exactly

If you're using a different printer, they will likely have their own specifications. Be sure to do your research and plan accordingly.

Don't Let Formatting Derail Your Launch

Formatting delays are one of the top reasons authors miss deadlines. Avoid the scramble.

Plan ahead:

- Build in 1–2 weeks minimum for formatting

- Order a physical proof (always!)

- Budget time for tweaks or file rejections

- Include formatting time in your launch timeline

Format Like a Professional

Your interior must be just as polished as your cover. Because after that scroll-stopping artwork pulls them in, it's the reading experience that either keeps them hooked or sends them running.

Ask yourself:

- Does this book look and feel like something a publisher would release?

- Is it as easy to read as a bestseller in your genre?

- Can it pass a bookstore buyer or librarian's sniff test? *Hint: You probably can't answer that yourself. Go ask a bookseller or librarian for their honest take.*

If not—fix it. Because nothing says "this isn't ready" like poor formatting. But a beautiful, readable page goes a long way toward a successful book.

Now that you've got polished book files, it's time to discuss how to take your manuscript from a computer file to a well packaged book you can hold in your hands.

CHAPTER 12

Packaging Your Book Like a Pro

You wrote the thing. You edited it. You're almost ready to publish. But before you upload anything, we need to talk about one of the most underestimated—and mission-critical—parts of indie publishing: packaging.

That's right: trim size, page count, cover type, spine design, back cover copy, pricing, and how your book physically looks and feels. It's the part many authors ignore until it's too late. But readers notice. Retailers notice. Reviewers definitely notice. Get it wrong, and your book may never leave the garage.

Think Like a Publisher, Not Just a Writer

Once the inside of your book is polished, it's time to look at the outside. Packaging is the visual, structural, and physical presentation of your book. It tells readers and retailers what to expect. If it doesn't match genre expectations or consumer standards, even a brilliant book will struggle to sell.

A well-packaged book:

- Looks professional
- Meets genre standards
- Communicates clearly to the right reader
- Complies with retailer and distributor specs

Choosing the Right Trim Size and Format

You might be tempted to model your book after your own bookshelf favorites. But ask yourself:

- Are those books in your genre?
- Were they traditionally published?
- Are they recent bestsellers or outdated formats?

Your personal taste isn't always aligned with what readers expect. Instead, look at what's actually selling in your category, starting with trim size.

At New Shelves Books, we track top sellers across major lists to see which trim sizes dominate. The following table shows the results.

Genre-Based Trim Sizes

Genre	Common Trim Sizes (inches)
General Fiction	5"×8", 5.25"×8", 5.5"×8.5", 6"×9"
General Nonfiction	5.5"×8.5", 6"×9", 7"×10", 6"×9"
Thrillers/Mysteries	5.25"×8", 5"×8",
YA Fiction	5"×8", 5.5"×8.5"
YA Fantasy/Sci-Fi	5.5"×8.5", 6"×9"
Self-Help	5.25"×8", 5.5"×8.5"
Inspirational/ Spiritual	5"×8", 5.25"×8"
Memoir	5.25"×8", 5.5"×8.5", 6"×9"
Reference	6"×9", 7"×10"
Middle Grade	5"×8", 5.25"×8"
Picture Books (PB)	8.5"×8.5", 8"×10"
Picture Books (HC)	10"×10", 8.5"×11"
Business	5.5"×8.5", 6"×9"

Choose a trim size that fits your genre and reader expectations. Avoid spiral-bound formats unless absolutely necessary as most retailers don't like to stock them because of their tendency to become tangled or broken.

Page Count, Spine Width, and Word Counts

A book's word count directly affects its page count, which in turn determines trim size and spine width. A trade paperback (5.5" × 8.5") averages 250 to 300 words per page, while a trade hardcover (6" × 9") runs closer to 275 to 325 words per page. Spine width depends not only on total page count but also on paper thickness, a detail your cover designer must have for accurate layout.

But page count isn't just a technical measurement. It's also a signal to readers. Too few pages and the book feels unsubstantial; too many and it can become costly or intimidating. To help you gauge expectations, here's a breakdown of typical page counts by genre:

Genre-Based Page Counts

Genre	Typical Page Count
Romance	250–350 pages
Mystery	250–350 pages
Thriller/Suspense	300–400 pages
Fantasy	400–600 pages
Science Fiction	300–500 pages
Historical Fiction	350–500 pages
Horror	250–350 pages
Adventure	250–400 pages
Young Adult	250–400 pages
Middle Grade	150–250 pages
Memoir	200–300 pages
Self-Help	150–250 pages
Business	180–250 pages
True Crime	250–400 pages
Inspirational/Spiritual	180–250 pages

Print Specs: POD vs. Offset

- **Print-on-Demand (POD):** Ideal for most indie authors. Cost-effective and flexible. Watch for compatibility differences between KDP and IngramSpark.

- **Offset/Bulk Printing:** Higher quality and lower per-unit cost, but requires upfront investment and inventory management.

Pro Tip: A file that works on KDP may not meet IngramSpark's specs. Match your layout to printer requirements and always order proofs from both platforms.

Material Choices: Paper, Finish, Binding

- **Paper:** Cream for fiction, white for nonfiction.

- **Finish:** Matte looks modern and soft. Glossy is bold but shows fingerprints.

- **Binding:** Perfect binding is standard. Hardcover adds durability and prestige but at a cost.

Designing the Spine and Back Cover

Books under 100 pages may not have room for spine text. For longer books, include title, author name, and publisher logo (if applicable). Choose fonts that are clear and ensure strong color contrast.

Back cover copy should hook the reader quickly. Start with an attention-grabbing line, follow with one or two compelling paragraphs, and end with a short bio or call to action (CTA). Study bestsellers in your genre for inspiration.

Barcode and ISBN Placement

- KDP provides barcodes.
- IngramSpark and offset printers require supplied barcodes.
- Embed ISBN and price in the barcode.
- Place in the lower-right corner of the back cover with adequate white space.

Strategic Pricing

- Base your price on genre, format, and production costs
- Avoid oddly specific prices like $17.42
- Use psychological pricing: $14.99, $19.95, etc.
- Rule of thumb: Keep total production costs below 30% of your list price

Design to Sell, Not to Please Yourself

You are not your reader. A font you love might be unreadable. That dragon illustration might suggest YA fantasy when your book is a literary memoir. Study the covers of bestsellers in your genre. Build a swipe file of fonts, layouts, and imagery that fit your market. Design for your reader first.

The Look of a Successful Book

Professional books share visual traits: modern fonts, smart color palettes, generous white space, and consistent layout. Back covers often include a short blurb, testimonials, and clean design. Aim for cohesion and clarity.

Packaging Prep Checklist

- Trim size matches genre expectations
- Page count aligns with market standards
- Spine width matches layout specs
- Paper, finish, and binding selected
- Back cover includes hook, blurb, and CTA
- ISBN/barcode properly placed and embedded
- Price set using comps and psychology
- Design files pass printer specs
- Printed proof reviewed
- Packaging reflects a professional standard

The Bottom Line: Your Book Is a Product

You poured your heart into the writing, but buyers will judge your book in seconds. Appearance, size, feel, and packaging all influence their decision. Give your book every chance to succeed by aligning it with professional standards. In other words: treat your book like a product, not a passion project.

PART III

Publishing Like a Pro

CHAPTER 13

Your Book's Journey: Distribution, Wholesalers, and More

You're not just an author anymore. You're a publisher. A business owner. A strategist. A logistics manager. And yes, you still have to be creative, inspiring, and disciplined enough to finish the actual book. Fun, right? Right? (This is where you smile, nod, and pretend this is exactly what you signed up for.)

That means mastering not just how to write a book, but how to bring it to market like a pro. If you've ever dreamed of seeing your book in a bookstore window—stacked tall, gleaming under the spotlight, with eager readers scooping it off the table—you're not alone. But here's the truth: the bookstore shelf isn't the final stop. It's just a scenic overlook. The real finish line? A reader's nightstand. And still in their head the next morning, long after they've closed the cover and turned out the light.

Publishing is a journey. And you need a map—one that includes both the scenic bookstore detours and the high-speed highway of online sales.

Your Publishing Supply Chain

To reach readers, your book must travel a defined path:

> **YOU → PUBLISHER → DISTRIBUTOR/**
> **WHOLESALER → RETAILER → READER**

In the pages ahead, we'll walk that route together, so you can see exactly how your book makes its way into readers' hands.

Step 1: You Become the Publisher

Once your manuscript is polished and ready, it's time to shift gears from storyteller to strategist. You're not just launching a book; you're launching a product. That means finalizing your cover and interior files, registering ISBNs and barcodes, and choosing a print method: POD (print-on-demand), offset, or a hybrid of both. You'll upload your files to platforms like KDP and IngramSpark, set your retail pricing, offer wholesale discounts (typically 40–55%), and determine whether your book will be returnable.

Here's the catch: personal preference has to take a back seat to industry standards. Retailers and distributors aren't interested in what feels fair. They're interested in what sells. When it comes to things like returnability and pricing, your book needs to play by industry rules. That's how it earns a spot on the shelf.

And speaking of shelves: don't forget the financial reality waiting on the other side. Payments from retailers and distributors are slow—think 90 to 120 days slow. Returns can be brutal, especially if you haven't budgeted for them. This isn't a set-it-and-forget-it side hustle. It's a business, and your cash flow will need to act like it.

How the Money Really Works

Let's do some math. Here's what you actually earn:

IngramSpark Example (55% Discount)

Detail	Amount
Retail Price	$16.99
Wholesale Discount (55%)	-$9.34
Revenue to You (pre-printing)	$7.65
Print Cost	-$4.16
Net Profit	$3.49

KDP Example (Amazon)

Detail	Amount
Retail Price	$16.99
Amazon's Cut (40%)	-$6.79
Revenue to You (pre-printing)	$10.20
Print Cost	-$4.00
Net Profit	$6.20

Takeaway: Use both. KDP for Amazon, IngramSpark for everywhere else.

Step 2: Enter Distributors and Wholesalers

Authors often confuse the terms, but distributors, wholesalers, and print-on-demand platforms each play distinct roles in the publishing ecosystem. Distributors (like IPG or Cardinal Publishers Group) act as your outsourced sales and logistics department. They pitch your book to bookstores and libraries, manage warehousing, handle invoicing and returns, and sometimes offer marketing support. This full-service partnership typically comes at a cost of 25–40% of your net sales.

Wholesalers (like Ingram) function more like centralized databases. They warehouse and list your book in their catalog, making it visible and orderable by bookstores and libraries. However, they don't actively pitch or promote your title—it's up to the retailer to discover and order it.

Distributors vs. Wholesalers: Quick Comparison

Feature	Distributors	Wholesalers
Role	Sales + logistics	Fulfillment for retailers
Pitch your book?	Sometimes	Never
Who uses them?	Publishers, some authors	Retailers + libraries
Require marketing?	Yes	No
Control over terms	Sometimes	Rarely

Print-on-demand platforms such as IngramSpark and Amazon KDP let you produce and distribute your book without warehousing inventory. They also provide built-in distribution paths: connecting to wholesalers like Ingram and to retailers like Amazon. IngramSpark offers broader bookstore and library access through Ingram Wholesale, while Amazon KDP is optimized for direct Amazon sales.

Indie authors can't access Ingram directly.
Use IngramSpark to get in the door.

Step 3: Understanding Retail Sales Channels

Not all books reach readers the same way. Today's indie authors have three primary sales channels to consider—each with unique pros, cons, and requirements.

Wholesale and Brick-and-Mortar Retail

Retailers stock books they believe will sell. But taking on your book is a risk for them, and minimizing that risk is part of your job as a publisher. To be taken seriously, you'll need to offer:

- 40–55% wholesale discount
- Returnability
- Reliable fulfillment
- Polished packaging and metadata

Books that don't meet these standards rarely get shelf space.

And here's the kicker: with that visibility comes the headache of returns.

Returns are the industry monster no one wants to face, but

every indie publisher has to deal with them sooner or later. Most bookstores won't even consider carrying your book unless it's returnable, and up to 40% of those orders may come back— sometimes damaged and unsellable. That's the trade-off for broader retail exposure: more reach, more risk.

If you're using IngramSpark for print-on-demand distribution, you'll choose from three return options:

- **Non-Returnable:** Safer financially but limits your retail opportunities

- **Return & Deliver:** Returned books are shipped to you (you pay shipping)

- **Return & Destroy:** Books are pulped and you avoid shipping fees

Most offset print distributors offer similar terms. In fact, some require a returnable status just to partner with you for distribution or warehousing.

Booksellers order your book on a trial basis. If it doesn't sell, they return it and you get charged back the wholesale price (plus shipping if you selected the Return & Deliver option). The Return & Destroy option is usually the most cost-effective for indie publishers.

If the wholesale process described above sounds overwhelming or intimidating, you might consider trying consignment sales first. Not every store works with consignment, but many independent bookstores, gift shops, and even some chain stores do.

In a consignment setup, the author delivers books to the store and signs an agreement to split profits if the books sell. A 60/40 split is common, with the author receiving the larger portion. For example, if your book sells for $20, the store keeps

$8 and you receive $12. If it cost you $6 to print the book, your profit would be $6. However, some stores also charge a set-up or administrative fee to place consignment books on their shelves which can eat into your profits, so be sure to ask about terms up front when discussing splits and agreements.

Keep in mind that consignment is only practical if you're local or willing to handle shipping and manage the entire process yourself. It's not a good option if you're hoping for national stocking. But it can work well for local or regional sales, especially if you're doing events in the area.

Online Retailers (Amazon and Beyond)

Roughly 70% of print book sales now happen online, with Amazon taking the lion's share. For indie authors, that makes working directly with Amazon KDP for print-on-demand publishing a strategic move. Unlike traditional brick-and-mortar distribution—where books are printed in bulk, warehoused, and shipped to stores on a returnable basis—KDP titles are printed only when a customer places an order. Returns still happen, but they usually come from individual readers rather than retailers. The result is fewer returns overall and far less financial risk than stocking physical shelves through wholesale channels.

That said, KDP isn't the *only* way to sell on Amazon. Indie authors actually have four main ways to get their books listed on the platform:

- **KDP (Kindle Direct Publishing):** The most common path. Your book is listed directly on Amazon, printed on demand, and shipped to the customer automatically. Amazon takes a portion of each sale: 40% of the list price for standard print distribution, with the author also covering the unit's print cost. This royalty structure is comparable to what most other retailers take, but it's important to build it into your pricing.

- **Seller Central:** A marketplace account where you list and sell books you've printed in bulk. You handle inventory, pack and ship orders, and cover postage. This gives you more control over pricing and sometimes a higher margin, but it also makes you responsible for fulfillment. Amazon charges either per-unit selling fees or a monthly subscription to sell on their platform.

- **Through a Distributor:** If you've printed offset runs, you can work with a distributor who warehouses your books, lists them with retailers (including Amazon), and fulfills orders. This option is the most hands-off for authors, but it comes with the distributor fees mentioned in the last section, stacked on top of Amazon's standard retailer discount.

- **IngramSpark Print-on-Demand:** Amazon can also source copies of your book from Ingram (via IngramSpark) at the wholesale terms you set there. This ensures availability, but it's less efficient than listing directly through KDP. Books supplied through IngramSpark often show longer shipping times, may appear as "out of stock," and net you lower royalties after wholesale discounts and print costs. For POD sales on Amazon, KDP almost always works better.

Amazon may dominate, but there are other online retailers to consider as well. Even if you don't prioritize brick-and-mortar stores, keeping your book available through platforms like Barnes & Noble and Bookshop.org broadens your reach.

Distribution partners and IngramSpark extend that reach further by listing your title with multiple outlets, opening additional sales channels beyond Amazon's marketplace. And don't forget: online sales aren't limited to print. Ebooks and audiobooks provide extra revenue streams and can be sold on Amazon, Kobo, Apple, and other major retailers, either directly or through an aggregator like Draft2Digital.

Direct-to-Consumer Sales

Selling directly to readers—through your website, newsletter, or at events—puts the highest profit margin in your pocket. There are no middlemen. You control the pricing, the branding, and the relationship.

You can sell digital files with tools like BookFunnel, or physical books through Shopify, Squarespace, Payhip, or Etsy. The upside? Total control. The challenge? You're the storefront, the marketer, and the fulfillment center all in one.

Choosing Your Sales Mix

A smart indie publisher understands the value of all three sales channels: brick and mortar retail, Amazon, and direct to consumer. That doesn't mean you have to use them all. The key is choosing the mix that best aligns with your strengths, your audience, and your long-term publishing goals.

Step 4: The Reader Connection

All this infrastructure leads to one thing: your book in a reader's hands. That might happen through a bookstore shelf, an Amazon shopping cart, a download on Kobo, a BookFunnel link from your newsletter, or a signed copy you ship from your garage. Don't get stuck chasing one path when there are multiple ways to get your book to the people who want it.

In today's landscape, authors who build direct relationships with their readers—through websites, email lists, social media, podcasts, events, and more—can thrive without ever relying on retail. Of course, retail still matters. It builds legitimacy and helps with discoverability. But it's no longer the only, or even the best, game in town.

Choose the strategies that match your strengths, your audience, and your long-term vision as a publisher. Publishing is a business. Treat it like one, and that's how you'll get your book not just onto shelves, but into readers' hands and onto nightstands.

CHAPTER 14

Production Timelines and Publishing Schedules

Publishing is not instant. Every step, from editing to proofing, takes time. Mismanaging your timeline can delay your launch, burn out your team, or cost you preorders and press.

Why Timelines Matter

Publishing is sequential. Each task impacts the next, and without a plan you risk losing momentum or missing your pub date.

A good timeline:

- Prevents last-minute panic
- Keeps your team accountable
- Builds launch anticipation

Give yourself the time and space to do this right, especially if it's your first book. Rushing leads to sloppy edits, weak covers, missed marketing opportunities, and a launch that fizzles. A well-paced schedule gives you breathing room to make smart choices, fix mistakes, and build buzz before release day.

Here's a sample 8-month launch plan that maps out the key stages most indie publishers need to hit.

Sample: 8-Month Launch Plan

8 Months Before Launch:

- Final manuscript to editor
- ISBN assigned
- Cover designer hired
- Distribution method chosen
- Marketing plan begins

7 Months Before Launch:

- Editing underway
- Back cover copy drafted
- Price and format set
- Register with Bowker and Library of Congress

6 Months Before Launch:

- Copyediting
- Cover design nearly finalized
- Estimate page count

5 Months Before Launch:

- Interior formatting

- Metadata to distributors
- Proofread interior and cover files

4 Months Before Launch:

- Print Advanced Reader Copies (ARCs)
- Begin Advanced Reader or Street Team outreach
- Collect endorsements

3 Months Before Launch:

- Final tweaks
- Upload to printer

2 Months Before Launch:

- Register your book with the Copyright Office
- Books ship to warehouse
- Send advance copies to retailers

1 Month Before Launch:

- Books appear in stores
- Final marketing push

Launch Month:

- Launch!
- Engage readers, monitor listings

1–2 Months Post Launch:

- Follow up with press
- Start long-tail sales campaigns

While compressing the schedule is risky and not recommended, experienced authors who know the process or those working under unavoidable time constraints can use the following truncated plan as a model for a fast-track timeline.

Sample: 4-Month Launch Plan

4 Months Before Launch:

- Final manuscript to editor
- Cover designer hired
- Choose platforms and assign ISBNs

3 Months Before Launch:

- Manuscript finalized and formatted
- Cover finalized
- Proofread interior and cover files

2 Months Before Launch:

- Proofread interior and cover files
- Upload to KDP/IngramSpark
- Send ARCs
- Prep launch strategy

1 Month Before Launch:

- Order final author copies
- Register with Bowker and the Copyright Office
- Begin launch marketing

Launch Week:

- Promote across channels
- Track rankings and reviews
- Start long-tail sales campaigns

Publishing isn't a race. It's a process. Whether you follow a long runway or a fast-track plan, give your book the time and structure it deserves. A smooth production plan means fewer delays, better quality, and a more successful launch.

CHAPTER 15

ISBNs, Metadata, and Retail Readiness

Formatting and cover design may grab attention, but metadata, ISBNs, and backend setup are what actually get your book onto shelves—both digital and physical. These are the details that publishing professionals never overlook, and as an indie author, you shouldn't either.

If you want to make your book discoverable, orderable, and retail ready, it's time to get strategic.

ISBNs: Your Book's Social Security Number

The International Standard Book Number (ISBN) is a unique 13-digit identifier assigned to every format and edition of a book. Think of it like your book's social security number. If you publish a paperback, an eBook, and a hardcover, each version needs its own ISBN to be properly cataloged and sold through professional channels.

Here's what an ISBN looks like:

978-1-234567-89-0

Each part of this number has a specific meaning:

- **978** – The EAN prefix for books

- **1** – The country or language identifier

- **234567** – Your publisher identifier

- **89** – A unique title identifier for that edition

- **0** – The check digit, a built-in validator used to detect errors

The ISBN might not be glamorous, but it is absolutely essential for book distribution, inventory tracking, and retailer listings.

Many platforms, including Amazon KDP, offer free ISBNs. And while it may seem like a convenient shortcut, it's not a strategic choice for most serious authors. When you use a free ISBN, the platform—Amazon, for example—is listed as your publisher of record in databases like Bowker's Books in Print. That might not seem important until you realize that libraries, bookstores, and many distributors may see "Amazon" as the publisher and immediately decline to stock your book. You also lose some control. The publishing rights associated with that ISBN belong to the platform, not you, which can limit your distribution options.

Owning your ISBN gives you full control over your metadata, pricing, and distribution terms. You show up in industry databases as the publisher of record, which adds credibility to your work. Most importantly, you have the flexibility to publish across multiple platforms and update your publishing details as needed. If you're distributing only through Amazon for a one-off release, a free ISBN might suffice. But if you're planning to build a professional, scalable author business, buying your own ISBNs is the better move.

In the United States, ISBNs are sold exclusively through Bowker at myidentifiers.com. At the time of writing, a single ISBN costs $125. A block of 10 costs $295, and 100 ISBNs cost $575. It's an upfront investment, but a practical one if you're publishing in multiple formats or releasing more than one book. Better still, ISBNs never expire. You can purchase a block now and assign them as needed over the months or years ahead.

One important warning: never buy ISBNs from third-party discount websites. Not only is it against Bowker's terms of service, but it's also how your book could end up published under someone else's imprint ... something like *Bob's Bargain Books & Bait Shop*. Hard pass.

If you're publishing outside the US, ISBNs may be issued by a national agency. In the UK, visit nielsenisbnstore.com. In Canada, ISBNs are free through Library and Archives Canada. Australia uses isbn.nla.gov.au, and in South Africa, ISBNs are also free through the National Library. Wherever you're located, be sure to check your country's official guidelines. And whenever possible, register your ISBNs under your own name or imprint to retain full ownership of your publishing rights and professional identity.

Barcodes: Tiny but Mighty

Flip over any professionally published book and you'll see a small zebra-striped block: the barcode.

It may look like an afterthought, but this little graphic is essential for selling your book in physical retail environments and it needs to be done correctly.

A retail-ready barcode should contain:

- Your ISBN (top line)
- A price-specific code (bottom line), starting with "5" for US pricing

Example:

- Book price: $16.95 → Barcode ends in 51695
- Barcode ends in 90000? That's a generic placeholder—not acceptable for most retailers.

Why does a price specific barcode matter so much? Retailers use barcodes to:

- Track inventory
- Scan books at checkout
- Integrate with POS (point-of-sale) systems

"You don't need a price-specific barcode." That advice gets tossed around in Facebook groups all the time, but it's flat-out wrong if you want professional distribution or hope to see your book on retail shelves.

> **MYTH:** *"Barcodes with prices cost extra."*
>
> **FACT:** You can generate a proper price-embedded barcode for free using tools like Bookow or following the popular free tutorial on the New Shelves Books YouTube channel.

Distributors like Ingram, Bookazine, and major retailers such as Barnes & Noble will often ask if your book includes a price-embedded barcode. If the answer is no, your sales rep may hear a polite—but firm—"pass."

So, if your goal is to get your book into:

- Bookstores
- Libraries
- Airports
- Big-box retailers

... then a price-specific barcode is non-negotiable.

It's a small detail that carries serious weight. Do it right, and you instantly look more professional. Skip it, and you risk being dismissed before your book is even opened.

Metadata: How the Industry Finds Your Book

Metadata is the behind-the-scenes information that makes your book searchable, sortable, and sellable. It tells retailers, libraries, distributors, and search engines what your book is, who it's for, and where to place it.

Key metadata includes:

- Title and subtitle
- Author name
- Series name and number (if applicable)
- Book description

- Keywords

- BISAC (Book Industry Standards and Communications) categories

- ISBN and pricing

Each of these elements plays a crucial role in how your book is categorized and discovered. Strong metadata is specific, relevant, and aligned with what readers are actively searching for. If you use overly broad terms like "fiction" or "nonfiction," your book will be buried under thousands of similar listings. Instead, aim for precise, searchable phrases such as "cozy mystery with cats," "time management for working moms," or "YA dystopian romance." These match real-world search behavior and increase the likelihood that your book will be found.

Think of metadata not as a technical box to check, but as the first layer of your marketing strategy. From search results to library catalogs and bookstore databases, your metadata works constantly in the background to connect your book with the right audience.

BISAC Categories

One of the most important pieces of this puzzle is selecting your BISAC categories. These are standardized classifications used throughout the industry by booksellers, librarians, and distributors to categorize and recommend titles. Most publishing platforms allow you to choose two or three BISAC codes that best reflect your book's content and genre expectations. For a complete and current list, visit the Book Industry Study Group at bisg.org.

A Quick Note on Amazon Categories:

While BISAC is the industry standard, Amazon uses its own category system that includes thousands of niche subgenres. These platform-specific categories are important for Amazon visibility and sales rankings, but they operate separately from your BISAC codes. In this chapter, we're focusing on the classifications that apply across all major retailers and distribution platforms. We'll cover Amazon-specific strategy later.

Metadata might not be flashy, but it's powerful. When done right, it dramatically improves your book's chances of being discovered. When ignored or mishandled, it can render even the best-written book invisible.

> *Metadata isn't just a backend detail. It's the first layer of your book's marketing.*

Keywords That Work in Your Metadata

When uploading your book to platforms like Amazon KDP, IngramSpark, or Draft2Digital, you'll be prompted to enter keywords as part of your metadata. These keywords are essential for helping your book appear in search results and be discovered by readers browsing online retailers.

As part of your book's metadata setup, KDP provides 7 keyword boxes, and you should use all of them. But filling them in isn't enough; you need to choose the right terms. Avoid overly broad keywords like *"fiction," "fun,"* or *"inspirational."* These won't help your book stand out. Instead, focus on specific phrases your target readers might actually type into a search bar. Examples include:

- "second chance romance"
- "space opera series"
- "grief memoir for dads"
- "budgeting for solopreneurs"

The best keywords are specific enough to attract your ideal readers and common enough to be searchable. A phrase like "young adult fantasy romance" is likely to perform well. On the other hand, something too narrow or quirky, like "YA vampire mermaid dystopia," may not yield any meaningful results.

To find strong keyword ideas, study bestselling books in your genre. Pay attention to the phrases used in their titles, subtitles, and descriptions. Tools like Publisher Rocket can also help you identify high-traffic search terms, estimate competition, and refine your list using real data from Amazon. Keep in mind that metadata isn't fixed. You can update your keywords over time to reflect changing trends or shifts in your target audience. Refreshing your keyword list every few months is a simple but effective way to keep your book relevant and discoverable.

A well-crafted keyword strategy won't guarantee bestseller status, but it does increase your book's visibility. And the more visible your book is, the more likely it is to reach the readers who need or want it most.

Retail Metadata Sync: BowkerLink and Beyond

When you register your ISBNs with Bowker, your metadata is added to Books in Print: a database that bookstores, libraries, and distributors search when ordering books.

If you own your ISBN, you can update and manage this information via BowkerLink.

That metadata also becomes part of the ONIX feed, a standardized file format that helps industry systems share book data.

You don't really need to understand ONIX, you just need to know that keeping your ISBN registration and metadata clean, complete, and up to date is important to the ONIX system.

Pricing Strategy

Pricing isn't guesswork ... or at least, it shouldn't be. It's one of the most important decisions you'll make when publishing. The price you set sends a message about your book's value, genre, and audience. If it's too high, potential buyers might hesitate. Too low, and it could raise questions about quality or professionalism. The goal is to land in the range where your book feels competitive, appropriate, and easy to say "yes" to.

Traditional publishers approach pricing strategically. They look at current market trends for comparable titles, page count, production costs, interior features like color printing or photographs, and even the author's reputation or platform. You should too.

Let's say you've written a 300-page nonfiction guide. Head to a bookstore or online retailer and find five to ten books with a similar topic, tone, and audience. Write down their prices and page counts. Divide price by pages to get a rough average per-page value. Many nonfiction titles land between six and eight cents per page. Using that math, a 300-page book priced at $0.07 per page would be about $21.00. That gives you a logical starting point for your list price.

But pricing isn't only math, it's also psychology. You may find that pricing at $20.95 or $19.99 feels more approachable to your readers than a clean $21.00. Many buyers make mental leaps when prices cross thresholds like $20 or $25, so even small differences can have a big impact on purchase decisions.

It's also important to factor in who's buying your book and where. If you're writing for parents, teachers, or librarians—especially in the children's book market—you'll want to stay competitive with similar titles, which often fall on the lower end of the price spectrum. But if your book is geared toward professionals, corporate clients, or event attendees, a higher price tag might not be an obstacle at all. A book sold at a conference, for example, isn't competing with other books on a shelf; it's a take-away from your presentation, a reinforcement of your authority, or even part of a bundled sale.

That said, if your goal is bookstore distribution, you'll need to stay within industry expectations. Book buyers know what their customers are willing to spend, and they use pricing as one of many signals to assess a book's fit for their shelves. Overpriced titles are more likely to be skipped, no matter how good the content may be.

To help you get a sense of what's typical, here are current pricing benchmarks across formats:

- **eBooks:** $2.99–$9.99

- **Paperbacks:** $12.99–$19.99

- **Hardcovers:** $19.99–$29.99

You don't have to stick rigidly to these numbers, but straying too far from them—especially without a strong platform or niche—can make it harder to gain traction. Genre fiction tends to fall on the lower end of these ranges, while premium nonfiction or books with color interiors can justify higher prices.

One final note: don't reverse-engineer your price based on how much you want to make per book. That's not how publishers think. If you want better margins, consider lowering production costs, selling direct, or using tiered pricing across formats.

> *Your readers don't care about your royalty rate. They care about whether your book is worth the asking price.*

Smart pricing is a strategic decision, not an emotional one. Do your homework, look at the market, know your audience, and price your book with purpose.

Wholesale Discount and Returnability

If you want bookstores to even consider stocking your book, you'll need to offer a standard wholesale discount (typically 40–55% off the retail price) and allow returns. Yes, as we discussed earlier, returns can be risky. But here's the hard truth: most bookstores won't stock non-returnable titles, especially from new or unknown authors.

I get it. This part of the business model can feel unfair. But in traditional retail, returns are the norm, and if you want to compete on that shelf, you have to play by those rules.

Getting Library Ready

If you want libraries to say "yes" to your book, you need to make it as easy as possible for them to stock, catalog, and shelve it. That means providing the same cataloging information they expect from traditional publishers.

Library Cataloging Data

Cataloging-in-Publication or CIP data is the classification block you see on a book's copyright page that is used by librarians for cataloging and shelving.

Here's the deal:

- The Library of Congress only grants official CIP data to established publishers with three or more authors.

- Indie authors typically don't qualify.

That's where PCIP comes in.

PCIP: Your Librarian-Approved Workaround

PCIP (Publisher's CIP) is created by professional catalogers and mimics the real thing. It includes:

- Library of Congress subject headings

- Dewey and LC classification numbers

- MARC records for library databases

Services like Cassidy Cataloguing and Quality Books offer PCIP packages for $100–$150.

PCIP information isn't required, but it is a value-added feature that makes your book library-ready. Even if you convince the library to buy the book, without cataloguing information it will often sit in limbo, unprocessed and unshelved.

LCCN: The Library of Congress Control Number

An LCCN is different from CIP. It's a unique identification number assigned by the Library of Congress to the catalog record of your book. Think of it as the library world's tracking number; it doesn't classify your book the way CIP does, but it makes it easier for libraries to find and reference your title in their systems.

Indie authors can apply for a Preassigned Control Number (PCN) through the Library of Congress's free online program. You'll need your ISBN to apply, and you must be based in the U.S. The number then appears on your copyright page, often just above where CIP or PCIP data would go. While an LCCN alone doesn't guarantee shelving, it adds legitimacy and signals to librarians that your book has been catalogued at the national level.

Retail Readiness Checklist

Use this checklist to confirm that your book's publishing metadata and backend setup are complete, professional, and ready for wide distribution.

ISBNs & Barcodes

- ISBNs registered in your name or imprint
- A unique ISBN assigned to each format (paperback, hardcover, eBook, audiobook)
- Price-specific barcode generated and placed on the back cover

Metadata Essentials

- Title, subtitle, and author name entered exactly as they appear on the cover
- Series name and number included (if applicable)
- Book description clear, keyword-rich, and reader-focused
- Metadata keyword phrases specific and relevant
- 2 to 3 accurate BISAC categories assigned
- Retail pricing aligned with genre and audience expectations

The Numbers Make the Book Move

Publishing isn't just about writing and creativity. It's about the systems that make the publishing industry work and this chapter is the foundation of your backend.

Respect the digits. They're the unsung heroes of your publishing empire.

Get your ISBNs. Register your metadata. Use the right barcodes. Set your book up for success. Because behind every bestselling book is a string of boring numbers doing very important work.

CHAPTER 16

Self-Publishing Platforms

You've written your book and created the files for publishing. You're holding the metaphorical key to your publishing future. Now comes a deceptively simple question: Where do you actually publish it?

There's no shortage of options, but choosing the right self-publishing platform—and knowing whether to go all-in with Amazon or distribute your book far and wide—can dramatically shape your success.

What Is a Self-Publishing Platform?

A self-publishing platform is a service that lets you upload, publish, and sell your book. It may offer printing, eBook conversion, retail distribution, and royalty payouts.

But here's what it's not: A traditional publisher. These platforms don't edit, market, or sell your book for you. You're still the publisher.

What Is Print-on-Demand (POD)?

Print-on-demand isn't just a technology; it's a business model that reshaped indie publishing. Instead of warehousing boxes of

books and hoping they sell, POD uses digital printing to manu-
facture books only when they are ordered.

This model reduces financial risk and minimizes start-up costs
for indie authors and small publishers. Whether you sell one copy
or a hundred, your book is printed as needed and shipped directly
to the customer. No upfront inventory, no warehousing drama,
and no truckloads of books showing up on your lawn

In the early 2000s, companies like BookSurge (later acquired
by Amazon and eventually folded into Kindle Direct Publishing)
and Ingram (via IngramSpark) pioneered POD technology.
Today, these two giants remain the primary players, with dramatically improved quality that rivals many offset printers.

The Benefits of POD for Indie Authors

- **Lower Financial Risk:** No need to front thousands of dollars for inventory.

- **Global Reach:** Your book can be printed and shipped
  worldwide.

- **Retail Access:** Connects your book to online bookstores
  and major wholesalers, often the only way to reach brick-
  and-mortar stores and libraries.

- **No Warehousing Needed:** Books are printed on demand
  and shipped directly to buyers.

And yes, the quality is finally where it needs to be. Back
in the early days of POD, it was a rough workaround. Covers
curled. Pages misaligned. The glue had the structural integri-
ty of a fruit roll-up. But thanks to major equipment and paper
upgrades by both IngramSpark and KDP, today's POD quality
has leveled up and if you've done your formatting homework,
most readers won't notice the difference.

POD in Action: How It Works

1. Sign up for IngramSpark and KDP using your publisher imprint.

2. Provide your tax and bank information.

3. Upload your print-ready files: interior PDF, full-wrap cover, and metadata.

4. Assign ISBNs (one per format) you own.

5. Set your retail price and discount structure.

Every time someone orders a book:

- The POD service prints and ships the copy directly

- The platform deducts printing costs and pays you the balance

- You receive reports and royalties based on actual sales

Meet the Big Players

Amazon KDP

- Print and eBook publishing

- Dominates online sales (especially US and UK)

- Fast payouts (60 days)

- Tools: Kindle Unlimited, A+ Content, Author Central

IngramSpark

- Best for bookstore/library access

- Superior control over metadata, pricing, and returnability
- Offset-quality POD options
- Access to Ingram's global wholesale network

Draft2Digital

- Aggregator for eBooks
- Distributes eBooks to Apple Books, Kobo, Barnes & Noble, Scribd, and libraries
- Has a print option that utilizes IngramSpark printers and distribution
- Free to use (takes a % of sales)
- Offers universal book links and basic formatting tools

Feature	KDP	IngramSpark	Draft2Digital
Print Available	Yes	Yes	Yes
eBook Available	Yes	Yes	Yes
Global Distribution	Moderate (Amazon-centric)	Broad (wholesalers + retailers)	Broad (wholesalers + retailers)
ISBNs Required	Optional for eBook, required for print	Yes	Yes
Returnability	Yes	Optional	Yes for eBook, No for print
Setup Fees	None	None	None

Feature	KDP	IngramSpark	Draft2Digital
Payout Schedule	~60 days	~90 days	~60 days
Retailer Access	Amazon only	Bookstores, libraries, online retailers	Bookstores, libraries, online retailers
Publisher Branding	Depends on who owns the ISBN	Your imprint	Your imprint

Decided on POD? You Will Need IngramSpark and KDP

The most common question we get at New Shelves Books: "Do I need IngramSpark if I already use KDP?"

The answer: Yes. If you want access to both Amazon's reach and bookstore/library markets, you need both.

Here's why:

- **KDP** is excellent for selling directly on Amazon. It has lower print costs and allows you to make more money per sale on Amazon.

- **KDP's Expanded Distribution** is not the solution it appears to be. It simply uploads your book to Ingram's wholesale catalog using Amazon's publisher imprint, not yours. That means less control, lower profit margins, and often rejection by bookstores that don't want to buy from Amazon.

- **IngramSpark,** on the other hand, gives you control over wholesale pricing, returnability, and metadata—essentials for bookstore and library sales. It is recognized by the book trade as a legitimate source.

Bookstores and libraries want to buy from industry-trusted wholesalers like Ingram. When you control your own IngramSpark account, you are seen as the publisher and not as "self-published via Amazon."

If you only plan to sell on Amazon, you can technically skip IngramSpark. But if retail stores, libraries, or international expansion are part of your plan, use both platforms and claim your space professionally.

KDP Expanded Distribution vs. IngramSpark

Feature	KDP Expanded Distribution	IngramSpark
ISBN Ownership	Amazon's	Yours
Wholesale Discount Control	Limited	Full
Returnability	No	Yes
Retailer Perception	Often flagged	Professional

Smart setup strategy: Use KDP for Amazon and IngramSpark for everywhere else.

Distributing Your eBook: Direct vs. Aggregator

When it comes to distributing your eBook, you have two options:

1. Sign Up Directly with Each Retailer

You can create individual accounts with platforms like:

- Kindle Direct Publishing (Amazon)
- Barnes & Noble Press

- Kobo Writing Life
- Apple Books
- Google Play Books

This approach gives you the most control over pricing, promotions, and metadata. It also means 100% of the royalty (after platform fees) is yours.

2. Use an Aggregator

Services like Draft2Digital allow you to upload your book once, and distribute it to multiple retailers. While convenient, these platforms take a small percentage of your royalties in exchange for the service.

Aggregators are a good choice if you value ease and speed over full control and are okay with sharing a portion of your sales.

Recommendation: If you want full control and are willing to put in an hour or two up front, direct setup is best. But if you prioritize convenience or have limited tech confidence, an aggregator is a solid option.

Should You Go Amazon Exclusive?

When you enroll, your eBook is included in Kindle Unlimited (KU) but must remain exclusive to Amazon, except for library licensing, for 90 days at a time. Enrollment auto-renews unless you opt out.

Why might an author consider it? Because roughly 91% of all U.S. eBooks are purchased or read through Amazon, and a large portion of that happens inside Kindle Unlimited. Think of KU as the Netflix of books: a subscription service where readers can binge without buying each title individually.

Benefits of Kindle Unlimited:

- **Lower Barrier for New Readers:** Subscribers are more likely to try a book by an unknown author since it's included in their subscription. This makes it a powerful discovery tool for debut authors.

- **Genre Popularity:** Kindle Unlimited is especially strong for voracious-reader genres like romance, fantasy, cozy mystery, and thrillers. These readers often consume multiple books per week and appreciate the value KU offers.

- **Author Payouts:** Authors are paid per page read, not per book sale. While the per-page rate is low (about $0.004 per page, though it varies monthly), the high volume can add up quickly. Some authors earn thousands per month through KU reads alone.

- **Double Income Opportunity:** Books in KU are still available for sale as eBooks. Non-subscribers can purchase them outright, and authors earn 70% royalties on purchases priced between $2.99 and $9.99.

Who Should Avoid KU?

- **Nonfiction Authors:** These readers tend to value and purchase information-based books more deliberately, and are less likely to binge content through subscriptions.

- **Slow-Releasing Authors:** If you write one book every couple years, the exclusivity might limit your income potential. KU favors authors with frequent releases or long-running series.

- **Standalone Authors:** Series tend to do better in KU. A standalone title might struggle without follow-up books to keep readers engaged.

Strategy Tip: Try KU for 90 days. Track your page reads, sales, and royalties. If it's not a good fit, opt out after the exclusivity period and go wide.

Going Wide: The Alternative

Publishing wide means your book is available through multiple platforms and retailers. It takes more effort, but offers:

- Diversified income streams
- Long-term stability and discoverability
- Greater access to global readers and multiple online retailers

Smart Indie Strategy: Hybrid Setup

The winning combo many indie authors use:

- **Amazon KDP (eBook + print)** for Amazon sales
- **IngramSpark (print)** for library and bookstore access
- **Draft2Digital (eBook)** for non-Amazon retailers and library distribution

This gives you the best of both worlds: Amazon's reach and visibility, plus broader access to non-Amazon retailers.

Upload Readiness Checklist

- ISBNs purchased and assigned
- Interior files properly formatted
- Cover fits trim size and specs
- Metadata complete
- Pricing and discounts chosen
- KDP, IngramSpark, and/or D2D accounts created
- Decision made: Exclusive with Amazon or going wide?

New Shelves Books offers free how-to videos and checklists that guide you through uploading to IngramSpark and KDP. Visit NewShelves.com/indieauthors for a full list of resources.

POD Is Great, But It's Not Always Enough

Print-on-demand changed the publishing landscape forever. It empowered authors to get to market quickly, test ideas with little risk, and scale up as needed. For the modern indie author, POD is not just a convenience, it's the infrastructure that makes a professional publishing career possible.

But while POD is ideal for low-risk launches and ongoing availability, it's not always the best fit for every book, or every author. If you're planning a major launch, need specialty formats, or want to maximize your per-unit profit on bulk orders, it's time to look beyond POD. In the next chapter, we'll explore offset printing—what it is, when it makes sense, and how to do it well.

CHAPTER 17

Beyond POD: Scaling with Offset Printing

Most indie authors begin with print-on-demand (POD) because it's low-risk and easy to manage. But if you're ready to scale your business, control your margins, or take advantage of bulk sales opportunities, there comes a time when POD alone won't cut it. That's when it's time to consider offset printing: the same method used by traditional publishers.

What Is Offset Printing?

Offset printing is the traditional method of producing books in large quantities—typically 250 to several thousand copies in a single print run. Instead of printing one copy at a time when a customer places an order (as with POD), offset printing involves producing a full print run upfront and managing the inventory yourself or through a fulfillment partner.

This method isn't for everyone. It requires more cash, more planning, and more logistics. But it also comes with real advantages: lower per-unit costs, more customization options, and faster access to books when you need them for events or direct sales.

Why Offset Might Be Worth It

Offset printing becomes a smart move when you're confident about demand. If you're planning to sell hundreds or thousands of books within a few months—say through a preorder campaign, Kickstarter launch, or a packed event calendar—offset can help you save money and increase profit.

It's also the go-to choice for special projects. Hardcover editions, workbooks, coffee table books, or anything with high design or color expectations will generally print better and more cost-effectively via offset. And for those who are growing a backlist and want tighter control over pricing and fulfillment, bulk printing offers long-term flexibility.

However, don't romanticize it. If you aren't sure you can move 500+ copies quickly, offset might just leave you with expensive boxes in your garage. Stick with POD until you have a plan and audience in place.

Comparing the Costs: POD vs. Offset

Let's look at a typical example. Say your book retails for $16.99.

If you're using KDP Print to sell on Amazon, you'll likely earn around $6–$8 per sale, depending on page count and trim size. If you're selling through IngramSpark to reach bookstores and libraries, your profit margin will drop to around $2–$4 per copy, due to wholesale discounts and print costs.

Now, compare that to offset printing. A 1,000-copy run might cost you $2.00–$3.50 per book depending on your specs. If you sell those books directly—to readers at events or through your website—you could earn $6–$10 per copy. That's a big jump in margin. But remember: that higher margin only materializes *after* you sell those books and recoup your upfront investment, which might be $2,000 to $5,000 or more.

Don't Fall in Love with the Fancy Format

I get it. You want a gold-embossed hardcover with linen boards and a ribbon bookmark. But unless you're about to sell 10,000 copies through indie bookstores next month, have customers lined up from a fully funded Kickstarter campaign, or your Aunt Doris has decided to bankroll your launch, it's time to be strategic.

Start with formats you can manage. Trim sizes, finishes, and page count all affect your cost and discoverability. Choose what aligns with your goals, not your Pinterest board.

Planning for Fulfillment

Printing in bulk solves one problem (cost) but introduces another: storage and shipping. Once you've got boxes of books, how do they get to your readers? Some authors go the DIY route, storing books in a spare room and shipping via USPS or UPS. Others outsource fulfillment to services like BookVault, ShipBob, or even Amazon FBA. There's also the hybrid model: use POD for retail channels (so Amazon orders are fulfilled automatically) and offset-printed books for in-person events, libraries, or direct-to-reader bundles.

Each approach has pros and cons. DIY gives you control but eats your time. Fulfillment services save time but cut into profits. The right choice depends on your business model ... and your tolerance for schlepping boxes.

But fulfillment is only half the battle. If you're printing in bulk, you also need to figure out how those books will enter the retail system—and that's where distribution comes in.

Distribution for Offset Books

Bulk printing doesn't guarantee bookstore placement. In fact, it often complicates it. To get your books into stores, you'll still need wholesale access, which you can achieve either directly (via IngramSpark) or through a distributor.

Distributors: Your Book's Sales Force ... Sometimes

Distributors place your book into wholesale channels and list it with key retailers. They also make it available to libraries, manage metadata, pricing, and inventory, handle returns and customer service, and sometimes pitch your book to buyers.

To work with a full-service distributor, you need more than just a printed book. They want to see a professional-quality product, a defined target audience, and a solid marketing plan. Distribution doesn't replace promotion. If your book isn't market-ready, a good distributor won't carry it.

Distributors usually take 25–40% of net sales and may charge additional fees. Notable distribution options include Independent Publishers Group (IPG), SCB Distributors, and Publishers Group West (PGW).

Choosing a Distributor: What to Ask

- How many sales reps do you have, and where?
- Do you attend trade shows?
- Do you specialize in my genre?
- What are your warehousing and admin fees?
- What kind of reporting do you offer?

- What is the contract length?

- Can I speak with one of your current authors?

Vet thoroughly. This is a business relationship.

Fulfillment-Only Distributors

If you decide you don't want to handle those boxes yourself but still want professional handling of your offset print books and access to wholesale channels, fulfillment-only distributors are a smart choice. These companies don't pitch your book, but they will store it, ship it when orders come in, and handle invoicing and tracking.

Fulfillment-only services are ideal for authors managing their own marketing but who want fast, reliable logistics. Expect fees in the 10–25% range of net billing, depending on the service level. These include Pathway Book Service, Itasca Books, and some packages through BookBaby or Bookmobile.

Wholesalers: The Warehouse Giants

Wholesalers are not distributors. They don't market or pitch your book. Their job is to make your book orderable by consolidating retailer and library orders and providing bulk shipping and billing.

The big players include Ingram Book Company (the wholesale division of Ingram Content Group) and Brodart (popular with libraries and schools). If you invest in bulk printing, you'll almost always need one of these channels in place to keep inventory moving.

The Offset Printing Checklist

Before you make the leap, make sure a few things are true:

- You have a sales forecast of at least 1,000 units, or a clear plan to move books through preorders, events, or direct sales.

- You've obtained a detailed quote from a trusted printer—and accounted for freight costs.

- You have a solid fulfillment plan, whether you're handling shipping yourself or working with a partner.

- You've set up wholesale pricing and returnability, and you know how your books will be distributed.

- You have a clear marketing strategy in place to drive demand for those printed books.

Offset printing is not the "next logical step" for every author. But it is a powerful tool for those ready to scale up and treat their book like a real product in a real business. If you've done the groundwork—built your platform, tested demand, and mapped out a strategy—then offset printing isn't just feasible. It's smart. And potentially, very profitable.

CHAPTER 18

Think Like a Publisher, Act Like a CEO

In this section, we're exploring the business side of publishing, because if you want to be a successful indie author, you cannot ignore the money, the math, or the mindset it takes to make this work long term.

Writing may be art, but publishing is business. If you are charging money for your books, you are not just a writer. You are a business owner. Welcome to entrepreneurship, whether you meant to sign up for it or not.

This chapter will not bore you with legal jargon or overwhelm you with tax codes. Instead, I will walk through the practical, sometimes uncomfortable realities of treating your writing career like a real business. Because that is exactly what it is.

Disclaimer: I am not an attorney or accountant. This information reflects common practices in self-publishing. For legal, financial, or tax advice, please consult a qualified professional.

Get Over the "I'm Just a Writer" Mentality

I see it all the time. Talented authors pour years into crafting beautiful stories, and then treat their finances like a hobby, until tax season hits or a big sales opportunity appears and they are suddenly scrambling to get their act together.

If your goal is to publish one book, hand it out to friends, and never worry about income, feel free to carry on. But if you want a sustainable, scalable career as an author, it is time to think and act like a small business.

Forming an LLC: Do You Need One?

This is one of the most common questions authors ask. Should you form a limited liability company?

The honest answer is: maybe. But probably not right away.

What an LLC does:

- It separates your business finances from your personal ones.

- It limits your personal liability if someone sues your business.

- It can look more professional when dealing with vendors, retailers, or collaborators.

What an LLC does not do:

- It will not automatically save you money on taxes.

- It will not protect you from bad reviews, negative emails, or imposter syndrome.

Most authors can start as sole proprietors. You can use your own name or file a "doing business as" name with your state. You will report your publishing income on your personal tax return, typically using Schedule C. You do not need to form a business entity unless you are using a business name or operating at a larger scale.

However, if you are earning steady income, releasing multiple books, hiring contractors, or building long-term assets like a course catalog or a speaking platform, forming an LLC can help you stay organized and legally protected.

Should You Form an LLC?

Question	If YES . . .	If NO . . .
Are you earning consistent income from your books?	Consider forming an LLC for better structure.	Sole proprietorship is likely fine for now.
Are you hiring contractors or freelancers?	LLC can limit liability.	Use contracts and track payments carefully.
Are you publishing multiple books or building business assets?	An LLC can help you scale and organize.	You can wait, but keep good records.
Do you want a more professional image with vendors or bookstores?	LLC adds credibility.	You can still look professional without one.

Pay Yourself Like a Professional

You are not your business. The business earns revenue. You pay yourself from the business.

Decide in advance how much you will reinvest in future books or ads, how much you will set aside for taxes and savings, and how much you will take as personal income.

This mindset matters. Do not blow your royalty check on impulse buys just because it feels like "extra" money. Your business needs cash to grow. Respect it.

> *Whether you form an LLC or not, you should open a separate checking account for your author income and expenses. Mixing personal and business funds is messy, unprofessional, and a red flag in any kind of audit.*

Naming Your Publishing Company

If you are publishing your own books, you should create a professional imprint. Do not publish under your personal name. Do not use Amazon's free ISBN and let them show up as your publisher of record. These small details can hurt your credibility with bookstores, libraries, and even readers.

Why It Matters:

Buyers look at the copyright page, the spine, and the back cover. If they see a vanity press or a name that screams amateur, your book is more likely to be rejected. But if you are publishing under a neutral, professional imprint like Avrock Press, Holland Publishing, or Capitol Books, your book is more likely to stay in the maybe pile.

Publisher vs. Imprint:

A publishing company is the legal entity responsible for producing the book. An imprint is the brand name used on the cover or spine. Larger publishers use different imprints to distinguish genres or audiences.

Most indie authors use the same name for both, and that is fine. What matters is how that name presents on your copyright page.

How to Choose a Name:

- Keep it neutral. Avoid references to pets, hometowns, or your own name.

- Make it sound credible. Think long-term and scalable.

- Search to make sure the name is not already in use. Start with Google, then check the United States Patent and Trademark Office at uspto.gov.

If it looks clear, you can begin using the name. For added protection, you can file a "doing business as" registration or form your LLC under that name. Then register your imprint with Bowker, KDP, IngramSpark, Draft2Digital, and any platform where your books will be listed.

Taxes and Bookkeeping

The moment you earn money from your books, you are running a business. That means:

- You must track income from all sources, including royalties, direct sales, and services.

- You must track business expenses like editing, design, software, and advertising.

- You must set aside money for taxes. In the United States, that means saving 25-30% of your profit.

- If you pay a contractor more than $600 in a year, you may need to issue them a 1099.

You do not need to be a financial expert, but you do need to know if your business is profitable. If you cannot answer that question, you are not operating a business. You are funding a very expensive hobby.

Use tools like QuickBooks, Wave, or even a detailed spreadsheet. And when your numbers grow, hire a bookkeeper or accountant who understands publishing.

Key Performance Metrics

If you want to run your author career like a CEO, you need more than a royalty statement. You need real insight.

Key numbers to track regularly:

- **Royalties per platform:** Where are you earning the most?

- **Cost of goods sold:** What does it actually cost to produce and deliver your book?

- **Ad spend vs. revenue:** Are your Amazon or Facebook ads paying off? Or just burning cash?

- **Email list growth:** How many readers are entering your funnel each month?

- **Readthrough rate:** Are readers buying your next book?

Use this data to evaluate your strategy. If something is working, scale it. If it's not, adjust. Guesswork is expensive. Metrics are your compass.

Copyright, Contracts, and Collaboration

Your book is intellectual property. That means it is a business asset.

- Register your copyright. In the United States, this takes five minutes and costs around $45.

- Read every contract before you sign. This includes agreements with freelancers, retailers, and distributors.

- Use written agreements for every project. Yes, even with friends.

You do not need a lawyer on speed dial, but you do need to protect your work and treat your business relationships like a professional would.

When to Hire Help (and Who to Trust)

As your publishing career grows, you may need help. This could include:

- A virtual assistant to manage email or social media

- A publicist to help with media outreach

- A marketing team to help with advertising and sales

- A bookkeeper to handle accounting

- A business coach to help you scale wisely

There are great people in this industry. There are also people selling vague and overpriced "done-for-you" packages. Ask for credentials. Read the fine print. Never spend money on services you do not fully understand.

Author CEO Checklist: Managing the Business Side of Your Publishing Career

Finances:

- Track all income sources (KDP, IngramSpark, direct sales)
- Track all expenses (editing, design, ads, software)
- Set aside 25–30% of profit for taxes
- Issue 1099s to freelancers as needed
- Open a dedicated business checking account

Legal and Structural:

- Decide whether to operate as sole proprietor, DBA, or LLC
- Choose a professional publishing company name
- Register your imprint with Bowker, KDP, and other platforms
- Register your copyright
- Use written contracts with all vendors and collaborators

Mindset and Growth:

- Set business goals and define success
- Reinvest a portion of income in your next release or growth tools
- Determine a pay structure for yourself
- Vet and hire professional help when needed
- Review your key metrics monthly to guide smart decisions

PART IV

Marketing and Selling Your Book

CHAPTER 19

Building an Author Platform That Doesn't Suck

Ah, the dreaded "author platform." Just hearing the term is enough to send many writers into a tailspin of anxiety and vague dread. If the phrase conjures images of a rickety wooden soapbox you're forced to stand on while screaming into the internet void, you're not alone.

But here's the deal: A good author platform isn't a megaphone for shouting "Buy my book!" It's a bridge. A solid, reputationally sound bridge that connects your work to the readers who are most likely to love it. And if you want a sustainable career, not just sales that fall flat after the launch party, you need one.

What Is an Author Platform, Really?

Newsflash: Your book is not your platform.

Your platform is your reach, your reputation, and your relevance. It is not something you slap together when your book goes live on Amazon. It is the infrastructure that supports everything else you do in publishing. The stronger it is, the easier it becomes to sell books, land interviews, get speaking gigs, and build the kind of career that keeps moving forward.

Your platform should work when you are asleep. When you are writing. When you are not launching anything. That is the dream. And it is achievable, but only if you build it on purpose.

A strong platform includes:

- A functioning, professional website
- An email list full of readers who opted in because they like you
- Social media that does not make you miserable
- Claimed and updated profiles on Amazon, Goodreads, and BookBub
- Public visibility through events, interviews, or guest appearances
- Relationships with readers, authors, booksellers, and real humans

Let's build it, one brick at a time.

Step 1: Brand Like a Boss

Before you post anything online or pick out a color palette for your website, you need to know who you are as an author and how you want to show up in the world.

Your brand is not just your font choice or whether you smile in your headshot. It is the promise you make to your readers. It is your tone, your topics, your values, and your personality.

Ask yourself:

- What genres do I write in?

- Who is my ideal reader?

- What do I want readers to feel when they engage with my content or books?

Then make some general decisions:

- **Name:** Are you using your real name or a pen name? Pick one and stick with it.

- **Domain:** Buy the dot com version of your name before someone else does.

- **Bio:** Write one that is short, relevant, and not filled with humblebrags. Be clear about what you write and why it matters.

- **Visuals:** Choose two or three brand colors and a tone. Are you classy, quirky, serious, lighthearted, niche, mainstream? Pick something and be consistent.

- **Photo:** Get a professional headshot. It does not have to be glamorous, but it should be clear, hi-res and no more than a year or two old. (Seriously ... your headshot should at least be from this decade.)

Step 2: Build Your Digital Home Base

Social media platforms come and go, but your website is something you control. If the entire internet collapsed tomorrow, your website is still your name, your brand, and your storefront.

At a minimum, your website should include:

- **Home page:** Who you are, what you write, and a simple welcome message

- **Books page:** Cover images, blurbs, buy links, and a few reviews if you have them

- **Contact page:** A basic form or email so people can reach you

Bonus: Add a blog, a media kit, or a press page later. But don't let perfection keep you from getting something live. A simple site done now beats a perfect one six months from now.

Step 3: Claim Your Online Real Estate

Readers, booksellers, and media outlets will look you up. Make sure they can find you.

Start here:

- **Amazon Author Central:** Add your bio, photo, and connect your books

- **Goodreads Author Profile:** Claim it and make sure your books are attached to your name

- **BookBub Author Page:** Even if you are not ready to run a deal, it helps to establish your presence early

Then choose one or two social platforms where your audience already spends time. If you write fantasy, Instagram or TikTok might work. If you write nonfiction, LinkedIn or YouTube could be better. The point is not to be everywhere. It is to show up where your readers are, using consistent branding, bio, and tone.

Quick-Start Social Media Checklist

- Professional headshot (no blurry selfies)
- Clear, concise bio that includes your website
- Business account set up (Facebook Page, Instagram Creator/Business)
- Profile headers branded with your book or name
- 1–2 active platforms where you post weekly
- Posts branded with a watermark, logo, or website QR
- Basic scheduling system (Meta Business Suite, Hootsuite, or RecurPost)

And yes, use the same profile picture across platforms. It helps people recognize you and builds trust.

Step 4: Social Media That Works

You don't have to dance on TikTok. You don't need to post three times a day. But if you want to build visibility and connect with readers, you do need some kind of social media strategy. And no, "strategy" doesn't have to mean "stressful."

The reality is that most authors waste time on social media doing the wrong things or, even worse, nothing at all. A little intentionality can go a long way. You don't need to master every platform. You just need to pick the ones that make sense for your audience and use them consistently.

Platform by Genre: Go Where Your Readers Are

Genre	Recommended Platforms	Why It Works
Romance / Dark Romance	TikTok, Facebook Groups, Instagram	Visuals, tropes, and fan-driven discovery thrive here
Women's Fiction	Facebook, Instagram, Pinterest	Ideal for the target demographic; personal content drives strong engagement and reader loyalty
Fantasy / Sci-Fi	TikTok, Reddit, Discord, YouTube	Fandom culture, serial storytelling, and fan theories abound
Mystery / Thriller	Facebook, Goodreads, X (Twitter)	Engaged reader groups and serial release followers
Historical Fiction	Facebook, Instagram, Pinterest	Visually rich content, strong appeal in book clubs and reels

General Fiction	Facebook, Instagram, Goodreads	Broad appeal across demographics, engaged reader groups
Young Adult / New Adult	TikTok, Instagram, YouTube Shorts	Strong BookTok and visual storytelling presence
Middle Grade / Children's	Instagram (for parents), Pinterest, YouTube	Reach gatekeepers (parents/teachers) with visuals and resources
Nonfiction / Memoir	LinkedIn, Facebook, YouTube	Thought leadership, personal storytelling, platform building
Self-Help / Business	LinkedIn, Instagram, Podcasts	Authority + engagement, especially through carousels and reels

Step 5: Email Is Not Dead

Social media is rented space. Your email list is something you own.

Email gives you direct access to your readers without the interference of algorithms. It is personal. It is permission-based. And it is still one of the highest converting tools available to authors.

To start your list:

- Add a sign-up form to your website

- Offer a simple freebie: a short story, a sample chapter, a reading list, or a behind-the-scenes note

Use an email platform like MailerLite, Kit, or Mailchimp. Substack can also be an option, though it straddles the line between email and social media. You own your list there to an extent, but the platform itself is still rented space. Then actually email your list. Monthly is ideal. Weekly works too. Quarterly is risky. Yearly is ghosting. Keep your emails short, helpful, or entertaining. Your goal is to connect, not to spam.

Step 6: Build the Foundation That Lasts

You do not need a million followers. You need a strong foundation.

Here is what that foundation looks like at the most basic level:

Author Platform: Minimum Viable Foundation

Element	Why It Matters	Minimum Requirement
Website	It is your home base and a sign of professionalism	Home, Books, and Contact pages. Optional blog or media kit.
Email List	It is direct and algorithm-proof	Signup form and lead magnet
Social Media	Helps with visibility and engagement	One or two platforms with consistent branding
Author Profiles	Improves discoverability and credibility	Claimed and updated on Amazon, Goodreads, and BookBub
Brand Identity	Builds recognition and reader trust	Consistent name, headshot, tone, and colors

This is not about becoming an influencer. This is about showing up with consistency and professionalism so people can find you, trust you, and recommend your work.

Start Local, Then Grow

You do not need to land on national media in your first year. Start where you are.

Reach out to your local bookstore or library. Join a local writers group. Offer to do a talk at a school or library or book club. Small, local wins help you build confidence, gather content, and create a track record.

When you pitch larger venues later, you will have something to point to.

Borrowing Someone Else's Platform

If your reach is small right now, borrow someone else's.

No, not literally. You can grow your visibility by contributing to existing communities. Some ideas:

- Guest on a podcast
- Write an article or blog post
- Swap mentions in newsletters with other authors
- Collaborate on giveaways or themed events

You are not taking advantage. You are creating collaborations that allow you to borrow someone else's platform while bringing value to theirs.

CASE STUDY: RUPI KAUR

From Instagram to International Bestseller

Few authors embody the power of a platform-first publishing career like Rupi Kaur.

What started as simple poems and line drawings on Instagram turned into *Milk and Honey*, a self-published poetry collection that exploded in popularity. Kaur designed the book herself and published through Amazon's Kindle Direct Publishing. Her fans, already emotionally invested in her work, made it a hit.

That success caught the attention of a traditional publisher, and *Milk and Honey* went on to sell millions of copies worldwide. Her follow-up book, *The Sun and Her Flowers*, only expanded her reach.

Kaur didn't start with a deal. She started with a platform. She posted authentically. She built trust. She delivered a unique aesthetic. And she made sure her book was well-produced, giving it the opportunity to grow into a bestseller once readers discovered it.

Her journey proves:

- You can build a global brand through social-first engagement.

- Creative control isn't a barrier, but it can be a superpower.

- A strong platform can reverse the traditional publishing process: readers first, publishers second.

You don't have to write poetry or be an artist to learn from Rupi Kaur. But if you've got a voice, a visual style, and the consistency to show up online, your platform can become your strongest asset.

Author Platform Starter Checklist

Use this list to make sure you are building a foundation that will support your long-term author career.

Branding

- I have chosen a consistent author name (real or pen).
- I have written a professional, relevant author bio.
- I have selected two or three brand colors and a tone.
- I have a current headshot that matches my author brand.

Website

- My website is live with a homepage, books page, and contact page.
- I have added an email sign-up form.
- I have secured my domain name.

Email List

- I am using a professional email platform (MailerLite, Kit, etc.).
- I have created a lead magnet to encourage signups.
- I email my list regularly (at least once a month).

Social Media and Author Profiles

- I have claimed and updated:
  - ° Amazon Author Central
  - ° Goodreads Author Profile
  - ° BookBub Author Page
- I am active on one or two platforms where my audience spends time.
- My social profiles are consistent in tone, image, and bio.

Community and Visibility

- I have engaged with my local community (bookstore, library, group).
- I have looked for a collaboration, guest appearance, or author partnership.

Build the Bridge

You do not have to love building your platform. You just have to do it.

A great book that no one sees will not get read, reviewed, or recommended. Your platform is not a gimmick. It is the bridge between your work and your readers. The stronger and more intentional that bridge, the further your career can go.

Start simple. Start small. But start. In the next chapter, we will focus on growing that platform through professional engagement and real-world visibility without losing your soul—or your mind—in the process.

CHAPTER 20

Marketing That Actually Works

I'm going to rip off the Band-Aid quickly: Marketing is not optional.

I know. You wrote a good book. You published it properly. You even bought the hardcover upgrade. Shouldn't that be enough?

No. And I'm sorry.

The book world isn't a field of dreams. It's more like an overcrowded flea market where everyone's shouting about their wares, and no one brought deodorant. If you want your book to stand out, you're going to have to market it like you mean it.

Hope Is Not a Strategy

Your book is not a beacon. It's not magically lighting up on some cosmic radar every time a reader thinks, "I wish someone would write a steamy slow-burn thriller set in 14th-century Wales."

Without marketing, your book is invisible. That's the hard truth.

I have seen brilliant books sink without a trace because their authors thought "great writing" was enough. Spoiler alert: it's not. The most successful authors aren't always the most talented.

They're the ones who figured out how to connect with readers and sell their work consistently.

The Three Pillars of Book Marketing

Real book marketing is built on three unshakable pillars: visibility, connection, and conversion.

- **Visibility** means readers can actually find you and your book.

- **Connection** is the sense that readers know you, like you, or trust your voice.

- **Conversion** is when readers take action: buying your book, subscribing to your newsletter, or leaving a review.

Every marketing effort should support one or more of these pillars. If it doesn't, it might be busywork. Or worse, it might be hope marketing.

Hope Marketing vs. Strategic Marketing

Hope marketing looks like posting "Buy my book!" twenty times a day, pasting your Amazon link in every Facebook group you can find, and praying that somehow, miraculously, strangers will trip over your listing and fall in love.

Strategic marketing is slower. Smarter. Focused.

It starts by identifying exactly who your readers are. Then it builds long-term visibility through email, social media, advertising, and media. Strategic marketing offers consistent value and clear reasons for readers to engage with you.

Marketing isn't about shouting. It's about inviting. Stop spamming. Start attracting.

Start With Your Audience

The best marketing starts before the book is even written. Who are you writing for? What do they want? Where do they spend time online?

Think beyond demographics. What problem does your book solve? What emotion does it deliver? How does it make your reader feel seen?

Define your ideal reader. Speak directly to them. Craft messaging that makes them feel like you wrote the book just for them.

Own Your Channels

Social media is helpful, but unreliable. Algorithms change. Platforms fade. Your email list and website are assets you control.

Your email list should have a welcome sequence that introduces you, your books, and what to expect. Offer a lead magnet—a free story, checklist, or sample chapter—and reach out regularly, whether that's once a month or every other week.

Your website should include buy links, sample chapters or bonus content, an author bio and headshot, and a basic press kit or events calendar. This is your professional home base.

Social Media With a Purpose

Use social media strategically, not constantly. Pick one or two platforms you enjoy and where your readers hang out.

Don't just broadcast announcements. Engage. Show up. Be human. And follow the 80/20 rule: make 80% of your content fun, engaging, or helpful. That means behind-the-scenes looks at your writing life, reader polls, quotes or excerpts, memes, milestones, or personal updates. Only 20% of your posts should directly pitch your book.

You're building connection, not chasing virality.

Launch vs. Long Game

A strong launch is great, but your book's success doesn't end at midnight on release day. In fact, most indie authors sell more books after launch than during it.

Launch marketing includes preorder bonuses, ARC campaigns, podcast or media appearances, and paid ads through platforms like Amazon, Facebook, or BookBub.

Long-term marketing includes newsletter swaps, seasonal promos, ongoing ad campaigns, and local partnerships with libraries, bookstores, or community groups.

Plan for both. Build for both. Success is cumulative.

Plan Your Marketing Like a Boss

Professional authors don't treat marketing as a launch-week scramble. They treat it as part of the job. Because consistency wins.

To make it easier, I have made the New Shelves Books Printable Marketing Checklist, available as a free download. It's designed to help you stay visible all year long without burning out.

Inside, you'll find daily, weekly, monthly, and quarterly marketing tasks, plus author platform essentials and realistic steps even busy writers can follow.

Download your copy at NewShelves.com/indieauthors.

And don't just download it. Use it. Add recurring calendar reminders. Momentum is built in the margins.

Paid Ads: Start Smart

Ads won't fix a broken book, but they will amplify a good one. Make sure you've got a strong cover, a compelling description, and a few honest reviews first.

Then test the waters. Amazon Ads are a good place to begin. Start with Sponsored Products and auto-targeting. Let your ads run for a week, collect data, and then refine.

Facebook and Instagram ads should use genre-based targeting. Keep the daily budget modest and test multiple images and headlines.

BookBub Ads allow you to target readers of comp authors. Track your click-through rates and keep testing combinations.

Promotional newsletters like Freebooksy, Bargain Booksy, and Fussy Librarian work best during launch windows or discount campaigns. Use them strategically.

Reviews = Social Proof

You don't need 1,000 reviews. But you do need some. Reviews matter. Good reviews build trust. Trust builds sales.

To get them, start by creating Advance Reader Copies (ARCs) that you send out to a select group of readers. These readers, often called an "advance reader team" or "street team," agree to read the book ahead of release and leave an honest review when it launches. These early reviews work to boost your visibility and credibility on places like Amazon and Goodreads, and they help build trust with future readers.

Your back matter—the pages at the end of your book, usually including an "About the Author" section, acknowledgments, or glossary—should include a short, friendly note encouraging readers to leave a review. Keep it low-pressure. A sentence like:

"If you enjoyed this book, please consider leaving a review online. It helps other readers find my book and makes a big difference to authors like me!" works well.

You should also email your mailing list and ask directly, ideally a week or two after launch. Make it easy by including a direct link to your book's review page. If you don't have a large list, or want to grow your reach, consider using platforms like BookSirens, Booksprout, or NetGalley to distribute ARCs and gather early reviews.

Don't beg. Don't bribe. Ask clearly and graciously. And be sure you're leading by example.

As writers, we know that the success of our book can depend on reader reviews. Yet, when I polled a group of authors, less than 10% of them had written a review for a book in the last 12 months.

There are plenty of excuses for why we don't take the time to review the books we read. Even when we decide to write a review, we might hesitate because we are unsure if we have anything worth saying or don't know how to post it.

The truth is if you can briefly answer three questions about the book, you can easily write a review:

- Did you like the book?

- What was your favorite part or most valuable takeaway?

- Would you recommend it?

If you answer the above questions and put the answers together, you can write a book review. And if you want readers to support you with reviews, make sure you're practicing what you preach.

Stop Guessing. Start Testing.

Selling books isn't sorcery. It's a process. And like all good processes, it improves with feedback.

Test different categories. Try alternate ad copy. Adjust your blurbs. Track what works. Repeat.

Marketing is part data, part heart. It's strategy and connection. When it works, it stops feeling like shouting into the void and starts feeling like building something real.

So take a breath. Make a plan. Start small. Keep going.

You, dear author, are not alone. You are the entire marketing department—with a gallon of coffee (or Diet Coke, pick your poison), a to-do list, and a book worth reading. Let's make sure readers actually find it.

CHAPTER 21

Mastering Amazon

If you're not optimizing your Amazon presence, you're leaving money, readers, and long-term momentum on the table. Like it or not, Amazon is the storefront of the modern book world.

And it's not just a popular platform. It's *the* platform.

According to internal data reported in 2024, Amazon sold over $16.9 billion worth of books in just the first ten months of 2022. That includes 456.5 million print books and 419.8 million eBooks in the US alone.

Amazon controls more than two-thirds of the US eBook market, and its dominance in print isn't far behind. This isn't just a trend. It's the ecosystem. So the question isn't *should you sell your book on Amazon*. It's *how well are you using the tools they offer?*

The Big Three: How to Sell Your Book on Amazon

There are three main ways indie authors sell print books on Amazon. Each has pros, cons, and best-use scenarios.

Sales Channel	Key Features	Pros	Cons	Best For
KDP	Print-on-demand, managed through KDP dashboard	Low overhead, "In Stock" listing, Prime shipping, easy setup	Limited wholesale access, Amazon exclusive if in KU	Broad availability, ease of use
Seller Central	Sell as a third-party vendor; manage own inventory and shipping	Higher margin control, flexibility in offers	No Prime badge, more manual work, "Buy Now" button not yours	Signed editions, bundles, direct fulfillment
Vendor Central (formerly Amazon Advantage)	Sell on consignment to Amazon; they manage fulfillment	"Ships from and sold by Amazon" tag, trusted seller listing	55% discount, inventory management, onboarding required	Maximum visibility, low-maintenance fulfillment

Important: If you're working with a distributor, they may handle Amazon listing and fulfillment for you.

Your Amazon Author Central Page

Amazon Author Central is your author homepage inside the Amazon ecosystem, and it's completely free.

Think of it as your digital business card. When it's well optimized, it builds trust and gives potential readers and industry professionals a clear picture of who you are and what you offer.

You can:

- Add a professional author photo and multilingual bio
- Claim and organize your books

- Track your sales rank and customer reviews

- View print sales estimates through BookScan (not real-time, and only partial)

- Add editorial reviews and cross-promote other titles

If your Author Central page is blank, it looks like you don't take your career seriously. Fill it out.

Amazon A+ Content: Boosting Credibility and Conversions

Amazon A+ Content allows you to add enhanced visuals, product comparison charts, custom images, and more detailed information to your book's product page. Think of it as a digital brochure embedded in your listing.

With A+ Content, you can:

- Create a visual brand experience across your book catalog

- Add graphics, quotes, and images that reinforce your message

- Showcase your series and cross-promote titles

- Help readers understand your value proposition at a glance

A+ Content is currently available to authors who publish through KDP and meet certain eligibility requirements, such as being brand registered or part of Amazon's invitation-only programs.

It won't fix a bad book or cover, but if your core assets are strong, A+ Content can keep readers engaged longer and turn more browsers into buyers.

Amazon Ads: What Actually Works (and What Doesn't)

Amazon ads are not optional if you want visibility in a crowded market, but they're also not magic. The best Amazon Ads strategies start with a good book, a strong listing, and a patient mindset.

Ads allow you to buy space in search results, on product pages, and even on Kindle devices.

Books that tend to perform well:

- Book one in a series
- Genre fiction with a loyal readership (romance, thriller, fantasy, etc.)
- Nonfiction tied to a specific outcome or trend
- Titles with professional covers, solid descriptions, and 10 to 15 or more reviews

How to begin:

- Use Sponsored Product Ads with automatic targeting to start
- Set a daily budget ($5-$10 per day is a reasonable entry point)
- Let your ads run for at least 7 to 10 days before tweaking
- Monitor key stats like cost-per-click and conversions over time

> *The first month of advertising is about buying data and learning what works. Don't expect an instant return on investment.*

Amazon Attribution: Your Secret Sales Signal

Amazon Attribution lets you track exactly how off-Amazon promotions like emails, social posts, or social media ads drive clicks and purchases. It's a behind-the-scenes view of your sales funnel.

Here's what it tracks:

- Link clicks
- Page views
- Kindle Page Reads
- Actual purchases

You generate custom links through your Amazon Ads dashboard, then use them in newsletters, online promotions, or interviews. This way, you stop guessing which efforts are working and start making smarter decisions.

Note: Amazon Attribution is currently available to authors in the US and select international territories only.

Optimize Your Product Page for Sales

Even with great ads, a weak book page won't convert. Readers make snap decisions based on layout, visuals, and copy. Treat your product page like your storefront window.

Amazon Listing Optimization Checklist

- **High-quality cover:** Professional, genre-appropriate, and clear even as a thumbnail
- **Strong book description:** Short paragraphs, scannable with bold headers, clear reader benefit
- **Thoughtful keywords:** Chosen based on reader behavior, not just genre or theme
- **Targeted categories:** Selected strategically in KDP; limited to three options as of 2023
- **Editorial reviews:** Include blurbs from credible sources when available
- **Professional author bio:** Optimized for trust and relevance, with a clear voice
- **Amazon Author Central page:** Fully set up with bio, photos, claimed titles, and updates
- **Amazon A+ Content:** Visual branding, book comparisons, or enhanced sales copy
- **Consistent pricing strategy:** Aligned with reader expectations and tested against sales data

> Important Update on Categories: Amazon no longer allows authors to request up to 10 categories via Author Central. As of 2023, you may only choose three categories, and only from the dropdown options provided within your KDP dashboard. If you're using a distributor, they'll assign categories via BISAC codes, so choose those carefully.

Reviews Matter: How to Get and Use Them

Reviews are social proof. They affect buyer behavior, ad performance, and conversion rates.

To leave a review on Amazon, a customer must:

- Have an active Amazon account in good standing
- Have spent at least 50 dollars on physical or digital goods in the past 12 months (subscriptions do not count)

Your reviewers do not need to have purchased the book on Amazon. Borrowed from a library? Got a free review copy? No problem—as long as they've read the book.

Amazon prohibits:

- Paying for reviews with money, gifts, or even free books if a positive review is required
- Review swapping with other authors
- Reviews from people with a financial or personal interest in the book (family, staff, contractors)

How to ethically get reviews:

- Include a review request in your back matter
- Email your ARC or launch team with a polite ask
- Use vetted services that distribute advance copies to real readers
- Follow up with readers who've emailed you praise and ask if they'll leave a review

Aim for a slow, steady stream of honest reviews. Ten to twenty good reviews can dramatically increase credibility and sales.

Amazon Isn't the Whole Game, But It Is the Playing Field

You don't have to love Amazon. But if you're self-publishing and you want readers to find and buy your book, you need to learn how to play their game.

And it's not about gimmicks. It's about:

- Clean listings
- Strategic pricing
- Strong metadata
- Measured advertising
- Ethical review building
- Enhanced branding through A+ Content

Amazon isn't just where people buy books. It's where they decide whether to buy them. That decision is made in seconds. Make sure you're ready.

CHAPTER 22

The Sales Materials Every Indie Author Needs

Before your book ends up on a shelf or lands in a reader's hands, someone has to say yes. That someone might be a bookstore buyer, a librarian, a podcast host, a book club coordinator, or a media contact. To get that yes, you need sales materials that do the heavy lifting. These tools prove your book is worth their time, shelf space, or platform. Professionalism alone isn't enough. You need to make it easy for someone to say yes to you.

If your book isn't selling, it might not be because it's bad. It might be because no one knows it exists. Visibility doesn't happen by chance. It happens when you show up with the right tools, make the right impression, and back your book with professional support materials.

Sales vs. Marketing: Know the Difference

- **Sales** is the act of getting a retailer, library, or organization to stock your book.

- **Marketing** is how you reach the end user—the reader—to let them know your book exists and is worth buying.

You can have the best marketing in the world, but if your book isn't available where your reader shops, you'll lose the sale. And you can get stocked by every retailer in the country, but if no one knows to look for your book, it won't move. Sales and marketing must work together.

Books are sold in many places: libraries, bookstores, gift shops, schools, corporate events, catalogs, online retailers, speaking engagements and anywhere else a reader might show up. Your job is to connect the dots between supply and demand.

Making Your Statement: The Who, What, Where, When, Why, and How

To create a targeted, realistic sales and marketing plan, start by asking (and answering) these critical questions:

- **Who** will buy your book? Be specific: age, gender, finances, profession, interests.

- **What** makes your book worth the price?

- **Where** will your readers find your book? Online? Indie bookstores? Airports?

- **When** will they need it? What life event or problem triggers their interest?

- **Why** should they choose your book over similar titles? (Be brutally honest here.)

- **How** will they find out it exists?

Once you've answered those questions, you're ready to write the two most important sales tools in your kit: your positioning statement and your marketing statement.

Your Positioning Statement

Your positioning statement isn't a summary of your book's plot. It's a business pitch: a 100-word explanation of who your book is for, why it's needed, and how you plan to reach its audience. This is what gets buyers, librarians, and publicists to take a second look.

Example:

Shut Up and Hire Me *is a step-by-step program designed for busy executives in transition. Each chapter takes less than ten minutes to read and applies real advice from Fortune 500 CEOs. Unlike other guides, it cuts the fluff and offers immediate action. Bill Billiam has hired top PR firm Blown Out of Proportion to promote the book and is the author of* Better Dead *than* Unemployed *and* More Money for Less Work.

Your Marketing Statement

Once you've clarified your position in the market, it's time to demonstrate how you'll get attention. Your marketing statement outlines where your book will be seen—reviews, ads, interviews, appearances—and by whom.

Example:

Shut Up and Hire Me *has been featured in* Business Week, USA Today, *and* MSN Careers. *It will be advertised in major-market newspapers and business magazines. Author Bill Billiam hosts the daily "Business with Billiam" on Fox 5 NYC and has secured a three-minute segment on* The Today Show.

Your Title Information Sheet: The Swiss Army Knife of Book Promotion

If you only create one piece of sales content, let it be a one-page title information sheet often referred to simply as a "one sheet." This single-page PDF introduces your book in a polished, focused format. It helps librarians, booksellers, event coordinators, and reviewers evaluate your book quickly. When done well, it gives you credibility and saves your pitch from the digital trash bin.

Include the following:

- Title and book cover
- A brief description (no more than 150 words)
- Key selling points that explain why your book matters now
- A short author bio, typically two or three lines
- ISBN, retail price, and available formats
- Ordering information, including distributors or wholesalers
- Your contact information and website or social handles

Your one-page title information sheet should be clean, visually appealing, and formatted for printing. Think of it as your book's resume. Keep it sharp, succinct, and focused on what makes your book appealing to the person you are pitching.

You will use this asset in a variety of situations. Attach it to email pitches, include it in printed packets, bring it to book events, and link to it from your press kit. It is one of the most versatile and essential tools in your marketing toolbox.

Sample Title Information Sheet

To help you visualize what a polished one-page title information sheet looks like, I have included an example below. This sample includes all the essential elements—cover image, book details, author bio, and ordering information—in a layout that's clean, professional, and easy to adapt.

Tough Love for Indie Authors

An Honest Look at What it Takes to Win in Self-Publishing

Anyone can self-publish a book. But publishing well—creating a book that sells and turning writing into a sustainable career? That takes strategy, persistence, and a deep understanding of the hard truths about the publishing world.

In *Tough Love for Indie Authors*, publishing expert Keri-Rae Barnum reveals what it really takes to succeed in self-publishing. Whether you're dreaming of bestseller status, aiming for a full-time author career, or trying to figure out why your book isn't selling, this book delivers the insights you need. Packed with hard-earned wisdom, smart strategies, and a healthy dose of humor, this no-nonsense guide will help you navigate the indie publishing landscape like a pro—without falling for shortcuts or empty promises.

YOU'LL DISCOVER HOW TO:

Succeed as an indie author • Publish like a pro • Market your books effectively • Run your writing like a business Open doors to agents & rights • Avoid common mistakes

This isn't another "feel-good" book with vague advice. It's a tough-love roadmap to building a sustainable author career through smart, strategic action. So if you're ready to ditch the "overnight bestseller" myth, embrace the work ahead, and truly win at self-publishing, start with Tough Love for Indie Authors.

Tough Love For Indie Authors: An Honest Look at What it Takes to Win in Self-Publishing

By Keri-Rae Barnum
Foreword by Amy Collins

Nonfiction, Writing Craft

Tradepaper | $20
ISBN: 9798897400065
300 pages (5.315" x 8.465")

Ebook | $9.99
ISBN: 9798897400072

Audio Rights: Tantor Media

ABOUT THE AUTHOR

Keri-Rae Barnum is CEO of New Shelves Books, a leading publishing consulting and marketing agency. A self-publishing and marketing expert, she has helped hundreds of authors build platforms, launch books, and grow lasting careers, and is a sought-after speaker known for her straightforward, actionable advice.

Sibylline Press • Publishing the work of brilliant women over 50 • sibyllinepress.com
AN IMPRINT OF ALL THINGS BOOK, CALIFORNIA, UNITED STATES | DISTRIBUTED TO THE TRADE BY PUBLISHERS GROUP WEST

CONTACTS

Vicki DeArmon, Publisher (marketing partnerships and events), vicki@sibyllinepress.com

Anna Termine, Rights, Licensing & Special Sales Director, rights@sibyllinepress.com

The Sales Packet: When You Need More Than a One-Pager

The sales packet is your expanded pitch. It is typically three to five pages and builds on your one-page title information sheet. Use this when you are pitching to regional chains, library systems, media outlets, or other high-level opportunities that require more context than a single page can provide.

A strong sales packet may include:

- A tailored cover letter or pitch message
- Your one-page title information sheet
- Your positioning and marketing statements
- Bound ARC, sample chapters or excerpt
- Praise or early reviews from readers or media
- Endorsements from authors, experts, or influencers
- Comparative titles with ISBNs
- Relevant author background or track record
- Highlights from your marketing or publicity plans
- A list of past interviews, appearances, or press mentions

A well-built sales packet presents you not just as an author, but as a professional partner. It signals that you are prepared, invested, and serious about building a long-term career—not just chasing a quick win.

Your Digital Press Kit: Be Ready When Opportunity Knocks

In addition to printed materials, every author should maintain a digital press kit. Whether it lives on your website or is sent directly to media contacts, your press kit is a ready-made information hub. It makes it easy for journalists, podcast hosts, bloggers, bookstore buyers, and event organizers to learn about your book and your background.

Your press kit should include:

- Author bio in both short and extended versions
- A high-resolution author photo
- A high-resolution cover image of your book
- Short and extended versions of your book description
- ISBN, format options, retail pricing, and ordering details
- Sample interview questions or discussion topics
- Links or summaries of past media appearances or interviews
- Clear contact information and your website URL

To streamline access, you can place your press kit on a hidden page of your website. Avoid making it a front-page item, but keep it updated with each new release or notable achievement. When someone expresses interest, you can provide the link with confidence and make their job easy.

Printed Materials: When Paper Still Has Power

Despite the rise of digital tools, printed materials still hold value. They are especially useful for in-person events, direct mail outreach, and meetings with local booksellers or librarians.

Situations where printed materials work well include:

- Author visits to bookstores or libraries
- Conferences, book fairs, or industry trade shows
- Targeted mailings to a small list of curated contacts

Start small. Order a short run of your one-page title information sheet along with bookmarks or postcards featuring your book. For most authors, a batch of 25 to 50 pieces is plenty to start. Test responses before committing to more.

Be selective. Do not send mass mailings to every bookstore and library in your state. Avoid impersonal packets or materials that feel generic. Follow up with a phone call or email after sending, and always honor each recipient's preferred method of communication.

Print should be purposeful, not desperate. Used well, it can enhance your presence and make a professional impression.

Email Pitches That Actually Get Read

Whether you're pitching a podcast, reaching out to a journalist, or offering a story idea to local or national media, email is often your first (and sometimes only) opportunity to make a connection. Inboxes are crowded, and attention spans are short. If your message is long-winded or unclear, it won't be read. A sharp, professional pitch, however, can open doors.

Use this simple format:

Subject line

Be specific and relevant. Tie directly to the outlet's readers, listeners, or audience.

- Example (strong): *"Local Author with New Thriller on Technology and Privacy"*
- Example (weak): *"New Book Out Now!"*

Paragraph one: Introduce yourself

Briefly share who you are, what you write, and any local or niche connection that matters to the media outlet or audience. Keep it short; two sentences at most.

Paragraph two: Introduce your book

Give a short summary that explains what the book is about and why it matters to the person you're pitching. Remember, this isn't your back-cover blurb. Think news hook, not sales copy.

Paragraph three: Make a clear request

Spell out exactly why you are reaching out and what you are asking for:

- "Would you be interested in an interview?"
- "May I send you a review copy?"
- "Would this be a fit for your upcoming feature on local authors?"

If you're pitching a bookstore or library instead of media, your ask might be: "Would you consider stocking the book?"

Attachment

Include your one-page title information sheet. Do not attach your manuscript, sales packet, or a dozen graphics unless requested.

Follow-up

If you don't get a reply, follow up once. If there's no response after that, let it go and move on. Stay professional. Do not spam, guilt trip, or beg.

Want your pitch to get noticed? Connect it to what the outlet's audience already cares about: current events, local ties, or your own personal expertise.

Your Website: Your Full-Time Sales Assistant

We already covered the fundamentals of building an author website in Chapter 19. That section was all about getting your online presence up and running—clean, simple, and functional. Your early goal was to create a place where readers and professionals could find you, learn who you are, and explore your books.

To recap, your starter site should include:

- A homepage that clearly says who you are and what you write
- A books page with covers, blurbs, buy links, and a few reviews
- A contact page with a working email or basic form

That's a great start. But if you're ready to use your site as a full-service sales and publicity platform, it's time to level up.

When you begin reaching out to bookstores, libraries, media contacts, and event organizers, your website becomes your digital handshake. It needs to support not just readers, but also the industry professionals evaluating you behind the scenes. It needs to show that you're not just an author; you're a professional with a publishing business.

- A press or media page with your downloadable one-page title information sheet and digital press kit

- Individual book pages for each title, with detailed information, formats, and links

- A speaking or appearances page, if you're available for interviews, events, or visits

- An email sign-up form for your newsletter or reader updates

- Optional content like a resources page, a book club guide, or bonus material

Make sure the site looks professional. Check that everything loads quickly, works on mobile devices, and doesn't look like it was built in 2004. Remove broken links, update old news, and make sure your newest book is front and center.

This is where people go when they're considering you for an opportunity. This is where journalists land when researching a story. This is where your pitch recipients click when they want to know if you're for real.

Your website is your full-time, never-sleeps sales rep. Make sure it earns its place on your team.

Website Essentials Checklist

Section	Must-Have Features
Homepage	• Clear headline with your name and what you write • Current headshot or branded author image • Direct navigation to books, media, and contact pages
Book Pages	• Cover image, blurb, formats, pricing, and buy links • Links to Amazon, Bookshop.org, and other retailers • Review quotes or awards, if available
Press/Media Page	• One-page title information sheet download link • Digital press kit with author bio, headshot, book info • Contact info and preferred media inquiries email
Email List Sign-Up	• Simple form with optional lead magnet (free chapter, bonus guide) • Link to privacy policy
Contact Page	• Email address or embedded contact form • Optional social media handles
Optional Extras	• Blog or article archive • Speaking/events page with availability details • Reader resources or bonus content

Look the Part, and People Will Take You Seriously

Your sales materials are your first impression. They are how book-sellers, librarians, and media contacts decide whether you are worth their time. A sloppy one-page title information sheet, con-fusing pitch, or out-of-date website sends the wrong signal. Clean design, clear communication, and easy access say something bet-ter. They say, "I am a professional. I know what I'm doing."

The best part? Once these materials are created, they contin-ue working for you. Every pitch, every follow-up, every inquiry becomes easier. You are not reinventing the wheel each time. You are refining it.

While struggling authors often hope their book will "catch on," successful indie authors make it easy for that to happen. They prepare the tools, build the platform, and show up ready to deliver.

These sales materials are how your book gets picked up, rec-ommended, stocked, and remembered. Make them count.

CHAPTER 23

Getting Into Bookstores

There's a unique kind of thrill that comes from walking into a bookstore and seeing your name on the spine of a book sitting on a shelf. For many authors, it's a career milestone. But behind that moment of joy is a complex, competitive process that very few understand when they first step into publishing. Bookstores are not magical havens for undiscovered talent. They are retail businesses, built on razor-thin margins, where every square inch must be justified by potential profit.

Indie authors can get their books into bookstores—both chains and independent shops—but it doesn't happen by accident. Success requires more than just a polished manuscript and good intentions. It takes strategy, professionalism, and the ability to approach booksellers as a business partner, not just a writer with a dream.

> *Success requires more than just a polished manuscript and good intentions.*

Shelf Space Is a Business Decision

It's romantic to think of bookstore buyers as literary tastemakers, selecting books based on prose and potential. But in reality, shelf space is a limited resource. Every book that gets stocked is a bet. The store is gambling that your title will sell enough copies, quickly enough, to make the shelf space worth it. Unsold books don't just sit—they take up space that could be earning money. For bookstores, inventory that doesn't move is not neutral; it's a financial loss.

This means your book's presence on a shelf must be backed by a clear reason why it will sell. That reason could be your marketing efforts, your local relevance, your publishing pedigree, or simply your genre's proven popularity. But the expectation is always the same: books must earn their place.

Chain Stores and the Corporate Pipeline

Chain bookstores like Barnes & Noble, Books-A-Million, and Indigo operate on a national level, with regional and corporate buyers reviewing book submissions months in advance of publication. If you've ever seen a holiday-themed table, a back-to-school endcap, or a summer reading display, understand that those displays were finalized well in advance. They are not thrown together. They are planned six months out, sometimes more.

The buying process begins with sales representatives from publishing houses—whether traditional or distribution-focused independents—who meet with category buyers and the retailer's marketing department. These meetings are scheduled ahead of each season and are tightly focused. Sales reps have just minutes to pitch each title, often grouped by theme, season, or marketing opportunity.

Marketing departments at the bookstore chain then weigh in. They evaluate how well a book fits the planned displays and whether cooperative advertising funds are available. Co-op, as it's often called, allows publishers to support books with credits that cover placement, signage, or in-store promotions. If a book doesn't have marketing support, or a publisher behind it willing to fund visibility, it often gets passed over.

What many indie authors don't realize is that without a distributor or sales team making these pitches on their behalf, their book won't be considered for front-of-store placement. Even more, unless the book is listed with a major wholesaler like Ingram, offers a full trade discount, and is returnable, it won't be eligible for shelf space at all. Retailers simply won't take the risk.

This doesn't mean indie authors are shut out entirely, it simply means the path is different. Instead of starting at the top, most indie authors begin with local independent bookstores and work their way up.

Indie Bookstores: Opportunity with Accountability

Independent bookstores may be more approachable than chains, but they are no less professional. These are usually small businesses with owners and buyers who wear many hats: managing events, curating inventory, running social media, and evaluating pitches from hopeful authors. Because they're more hands-on, they can afford to be more flexible. But that flexibility is often misunderstood.

A conversation with Beth, an indie bookseller in a small coastal town, revealed just how frequently self-published authors overestimate their appeal and underestimate what's required. She told me that she's approached weekly, sometimes daily, by local authors asking her to stock their books. Most of the time, she declines. And it's not because she doesn't support local talent. It's because the pitches are incomplete, the books aren't professionally packaged, and the authors don't understand the basics of retail.

One of her biggest frustrations is when local authors show up asking for her support, but have never shopped at her store. They don't attend events. They don't buy books from her shelves. They don't even follow her store's social media. Yet they expect her to take a risk on their book. As Beth put it, "If you don't support us, why should we support you?"

Her second red flag is a lack of genre awareness. When authors bring in memoirs or deeply personal nonfiction, she often asks what similar books they've read and how their book fits the market. More often than not, they can't answer. They haven't done their research. They haven't even read books in their own genre. That lack of context makes it impossible for Beth to evaluate where the book belongs in her store—or whether it belongs at all.

Then there's packaging. If the book's cover is amateurish, if the title isn't on the spine, or if there's no ISBN and barcode, she can't stock it, even if she wants to. "Customers expect books to look a certain way," she explained. "If it doesn't meet the standard, it won't sell."

The final nail in the coffin, according to Beth, is poor professionalism. Some authors respond angrily when she declines their pitch. They argue, insist, or guilt-trip. In her eyes, that's an immediate sign to steer clear ... not just of the book, but of the author entirely.

The moral here is simple. Independent bookstores may be your allies, but only if you show up prepared. That means professional design, competitive pricing, wholesale availability, and a respectful, relationship-driven approach.

Displays and the Economics of Visibility

Beyond stocking your book, indie stores may offer seasonal marketing and display opportunities, especially if you're willing to do the legwork. They're more open than chains to hearing your ideas for themed tables or a local author table. But remember, every display takes up space. It's not a gift. It's a business decision.

Some stores will ask for a small stocking or display fee, especially during the holidays or tourist season. While it might sting to pay for shelf space, think of it as advertising. A modest fee for a front-table display that puts your book in front of hundreds or thousands of readers can be a smart investment *if* your book is ready to convert that attention into sales.

The real goal isn't just to get into one store. It's to create a ripple effect. Each store you break into becomes a talking point, a sales opportunity, and a building block for broader distribution.

Driving Sales and Creating Connection with Events

Events aren't just about selling books on the spot, they're about building relationships. When readers hear you speak, ask questions, or engage with your story in person, they form a personal connection. Done well, a single event can turn casual browsers into lifelong fans.

Events come in many forms:

- **Solo Author Events:** Traditional readings and Q&A sessions work best when you already have a local audience or connection to the store. Include a brief intro, a few well-chosen excerpts, time for audience interaction, and signing opportunities.

- **Group Author Events:** Combine forces with other authors in the same genre. A "Local Romance Night" or "Voices in Memoir" is more likely to bring customers into the store and less pressure on you to fill the room solo.

- **In Conversation Events:** These pair two authors (or an author and moderator) in a more relaxed discussion about their books and shared themes. They feel more dynamic than standard readings and are growing in popularity.

- **Workshops or Talks:** If your book ties into a topic of broader interest—mental health, parenting, creativity, local history—offer a mini-workshop or educational talk instead of a sales-focused event.

The best events are structured, professional, and collaborative. Offer light refreshments, provide handouts like bookmarks or review requests, and invite attendees to browse the store. A well-planned event not only sells books, it deepens your relationship with the venue and the readers.

Professional Publishing is the Price of Entry

If there's one takeaway from this chapter, it's that you must approach bookstores as a businessperson. Your book isn't a passion project, it's a product. And the bookstore isn't your cheerleader, it's your partner.

Prepare a polished, professional pitch. Make sure your book meets trade standards. Know your comps, your audience, and your marketing plan. Be gracious if the answer is no. Be humble if the answer is yes.

Bookstores may not be the gatekeepers they once were, but they're still powerful allies in your publishing journey. Earn their trust, prove your value, and they might just give your book a chance to shine.

CHAPTER 24

Getting Into Airport Stores

For many authors, airport bookstores represent the ultimate dream in visibility. With thousands of travelers passing through terminals each day, the opportunity to have a book featured in these high-traffic locations feels like a major milestone. It's easy to imagine a business traveler or vacationer picking up a copy before boarding a flight, reading it cover to cover en route, and then recommending it to others. This aspirational vision, however, is far from simple to achieve.

Airport bookstores are among the most selective and commercially driven book retailers in the industry. Unlike independent bookstores that may consider local interest or support debut authors for community reasons, airport stores operate with a different priority: turnover. Every square inch of shelf space must earn its keep quickly and consistently. There is no room for slow-moving inventory, untested titles, or vague marketing promises. Success in this space demands a book that not only looks the part but has already proven itself in the marketplace.

Understanding the Airport Retail Environment

Stores like Hudson News, Paradies Lagardère, and other major airport retailers are not book-focused in the traditional sense. They carry a small, highly curated selection of books as one product line among many—competing for space alongside snacks, travel accessories, magazines, and last-minute souvenirs. The books that do get stocked are selected to appeal to a wide range of travelers, with a heavy emphasis on accessibility, entertainment, and portability.

The most successful titles in this setting fall into specific categories. Mystery, suspense, and thrillers are reliable performers across all regions and demographics. Women's fiction and romance also do well, especially in seasons associated with travel and leisure. Literary fiction is featured selectively, usually when supported by awards or critical acclaim. Inspirational nonfiction, self-help, and business books are also common, particularly in major hubs that serve a professional audience. Titles in these genres with national buzz or strong media tie-ins often receive priority consideration.

Books that do not perform well in airport settings tend to be those that require significant context to appreciate, those that are part of a series without a clear stand-alone component, or those that are overly long, academic, or niche in subject matter. Travelers tend to look for single-volume reads they can begin and finish during a trip, which means high page counts or deep literary complexity can be barriers to purchase.

What Buyers Look For

Airport bookstore buyers are not seeking fresh discoveries or experimental content. They are looking for products that sell. At New Shelves Books, discussions with regional buyers and long-time industry contacts confirm that the primary deciding factor for stocking a book is its sales record. A book with consistent sales, strong reviews, and a well-packaged appearance stands a far better chance of being stocked than even the most beautifully written book with no track record.

Buyers review data points such as sales velocity, online ratings, awards, professional reviews, and national publicity. They want to know that readers already want the book, not just that the author believes they should. Books with strong social proof—especially those that have sold well in bookstores, received media coverage, or generated significant buzz online—move to the front of the line.

But even with strong credentials, books must meet logistical requirements. They must be available through a major distributor, typically Ingram, with standard terms that include a full trade discount and returnability. The book must be printed professionally, carry a scannable barcode with pricing, and appear indistinguishable from titles published by traditional houses. Anything less introduces risk, and in this retail environment, risk is rarely rewarded.

Regional Appeal and the Myth of Local Author Advantage

One persistent misunderstanding among indie authors is the idea that being a "local author" will help land a placement in the airport store nearest their home. Unlike local bookstores, which may embrace community connections or spotlight authors from the area, airport stores are not motivated by geographic loyalty. Their goal is to serve travelers—not locals—and their product mix reflects that.

What can work in an author's favor is a book with a setting or subject matter that ties into the airport's location. A mystery set in Chicago may be of interest to buyers at O'Hare, or a travelogue exploring the Alaskan wilderness might be considered for Anchorage. But even this advantage is only meaningful if the book already meets the other requirements: professional quality, proven sales, and solid distribution. Without those foundations, regional relevance is unlikely to carry much weight.

Professionalism and Presentation

Every aspect of the book must convey quality. Airport buyers judge a book as much by its appearance as its substance. The cover should be genre-appropriate and visually appealing. The title and subtitle should be legible from a distance. The spine must include the title and author name in standard orientation. Interior formatting should look professional and be free of errors.

Trim size and binding also matter. Mass market and trade paperbacks are popular due to their portability. Hardcover editions are also common in business and nonfiction categories, particularly when paired with recognizable author names or publisher imprints. Oversized books, unusual dimensions, or unorthodox formatting raise red flags and may disqualify a title from consideration.

Books should also be priced competitively for the market. A paperback priced significantly above comparable titles will likely be passed over unless there is a strong brand or media driver behind it. Price-conscious travelers are unlikely to spend extra on an unknown author unless the book offers clear and immediate appeal.

Making the Pitch

Authors hoping to see their books in airport stores need to approach the opportunity with the same professionalism they would bring to a national publicity campaign. This means understanding the hierarchy of the stores and contacting the correct person. Most decisions are made at the regional level by buyers who oversee multiple locations. Store employees may be helpful, but they rarely have purchasing authority.

The best practice is to identify the appropriate buyer and make contact through a concise, well-prepared email. The pitch should include a brief summary of the book, the specific reason it fits the airport market, details about sales history and distribution, and a clear call to action. Attaching a one-page title information sheet that features the book ISBN, retail price, distribution information, marketing highlights, and endorsements can support the pitch effectively.

If meeting a buyer in person, such as during travel or a scheduled event, authors should be prepared with a printed one-page title information sheet and a copy of the book. However, the tone must remain professional and respectful. Buyers are busy, and airport environments can be hectic. A polite introduction followed by a quick hand-off of materials is far more effective than a long, impromptu pitch.

The Role of Stocking and Display Fees

Some airport stores may offer the opportunity to place a title on shelves or displays in exchange for a stocking fee. While this practice can seem controversial, it is a standard part of retail strategy, especially in high-value locations. These fees are not bribes or vanity placements. They are a way for retailers to test demand without financial risk.

Whether to accept such a fee depends on the author's goals. For those with an advertising or PR campaign focused on travel readers, or who already have strong organic demand, a short-term airport placement can be a powerful visibility tool. However, it should not be the first step in a sales strategy. It should follow success, not precede it.

Authors should also weigh the potential return carefully. Airport exposure alone does not guarantee long-term sales. It must be part of a larger, coordinated plan that includes reader engagement, online discoverability, and additional retail strategies.

Long-Term Positioning

Getting a book into airport stores is not a beginner's move. It is a growth strategy for titles that are already gaining traction, presented with professional polish, and backed by a clear plan. Authors who succeed in this space tend to have an entrepreneurial mindset. They treat their books as commercial products and approach every opportunity with the same seriousness as any seasoned publisher.

The path to airport shelves begins with foundational work: crafting a strong product, achieving measurable sales, and presenting that product in a way that makes sense for the audience. I regularly advises authors to focus first on performance in regional markets, independent stores, and online retail channels before pursuing airport placement. Once momentum is established, and the book proves its market appeal, the door to high-visibility retail opportunities becomes much more accessible.

Airport bookstores are not out of reach. But they are earned. With preparation, professionalism, and a strategic mindset, an author can position their book to take flight—quite literally— into the hands of readers across the globe.

CHAPTER 25

Getting Into Libraries

Libraries remain one of the most overlooked—and most power-ful—opportunities for indie authors. Sure, getting your book into a bookstore feels glamorous. But a bookstore might carry your book for a few months (if you're lucky), while a library can keep it in circulation for years. Think of it as the difference between a sparkler and a fireplace. One gives you a quick flash of visibility. The other keeps the room warm long after the launch party ends.

Getting into libraries isn't about luck or begging. It's about being professional, being discoverable, and being strategic. Libraries don't buy books out of pity. They buy based on need and demand ... and your job is to create both.

Why Libraries Matter to Indie Authors

- **Credibility:** A library purchase is a public endorsement. Libraries don't just toss any old book onto their shelves. If your book is in a library's collection, it's because someone with professional standards said, "This belongs here." It's like being recommended by the literary version of a trusted neighborhood elder ... quiet power that carries weight.

- **Discoverability:** Libraries are where readers go to explore. Patrons stumble upon new voices, new stories, and—yes—new authors. A reader who finds your book on a whim might just become your next fan, follower, and reviewer.

- **Longevity:** Libraries keep books on shelves for years, not weeks. Unlike bookstores, which rotate inventory quickly, libraries keep good books circulating. Your book might be discovered two years after its release and still make an impact.

- **Ripple Effect:** A well-placed library book can spark surprising results. A librarian might choose it for a book club, a teacher might recommend it to students, or a patron might ask a bookstore to order their own copy. Librarians are trusted community voices. Win one over, and they'll do more for your book than almost any other type of marketing ever could.

The bottom line? Libraries aren't fast money, but they're smart strategy. They are the slow burn that builds long-term careers.

What Libraries Require

Most public libraries purchase books through wholesalers, primarily Ingram Library Services. If your print book is available through IngramSpark, you're already checking a major box. Libraries like easy. They want to order through the systems they already use, not navigate custom requests.

And despite what some old-school publishing blogs may tell you, libraries don't care about offering a 40% wholesale discount or whether your book is returnable. That's a bookstore game. Libraries buy a book once and keep it. What they do care about is this: is your book catalogable, professional-looking, and relevant to their patrons?

That means:

- A real ISBN (from Bowker, not the free KDP one)

- Complete metadata (title, author, categories, etc.)

- Ideally a PCIP block and MARC record, which help their cataloging systems play nicely with your book.

Library Requirements and Distribution Table

Requirement	Why It Matters	Notes
Professional ISBN and metadata	Ensures libraries can catalog and manage your book within their systems	Buy ISBNs from Bowker and fill in metadata on distribution platforms
Available via Ingram	Simplifies ordering and ensures compatibility with library systems	Use IngramSpark to make your book available to libraries for print purchase
Clean, well-designed packaging	Improves perceived value and reader appeal; libraries expect professional quality	Hire a designer and formatter to meet publishing standards
Reviewed in trade journals	Boosts credibility and helps acquisitions librarians justify purchasing	Submit to Kirkus Indie, Foreword Reviews, or Booklife
Local or regional relevance	Increases relevance to local communities; many libraries prioritize local content	Mention local ties in your pitch and marketing materials
eBook availability	Many libraries now circulate eBooks to meet patron demand	Distribute through Draft2Digital or PublishDrive for OverDrive access
Audiobook availability	Audiobooks are popular with patrons and expand accessibility options	Consider Voices by INaudio or similar distributors to reach library audiobook platforms

Donating to Libraries the Right Way

Dropping a copy of your book at the front desk with a hopeful smile might feel productive, but here's what often happens next: it gets tossed into the donation bin, then sold for fifty cents at the library's annual fundraiser. That's not shelf space; it's a garage sale.

If you want your donation to count, be strategic. Make an appointment with the acquisitions librarian (or collection development manager, depending on the library). Hand them a finished copy of your book and a polished one-page title information sheet that includes your title, ISBN, availability (IngramSpark, please!), and contact info. This shows you understand how the process works.

Ask questions like:

- How do you evaluate new titles?
- Do you accept author donations?
- Should I follow up with the regional buying office or Friends of the Library group?

The key is not just dropping off your book, it's getting a decision-maker to actually consider it.

Sample Library Pitch Cover Letter

Want to make a strong first impression? Here's a professional, author-friendly template you can customize for your own library outreach. Pair this with a copy of your book and a polished one-page title information sheet, and you'll look like a pro from the start.

Library Cover Letter Template

Dear NAME OF ACQUISION LIBRARIAN,

My name is YOUR NAME, I am the author of a CATEGORY book that I was hoping you would consider stocking in your library as a print book and an eBook.

We are about to launch a marketing campaign and I'm contacting libraries to let them know that there will be some demand during and after this campaign.

NAME OF BOOK (ISBN: 978-XXXXXXXXX) is a book that XXXXXXX.

Once the marketing campaign begins, we will be directing readers to the libraries that agreed to stock it; so if you're willing, I'd like to know what terms and wholesalers you prefer when acquiring books.

NAME OF BOOK is available at LIST WHOLESALERS fully returnable at the full discount. The eBook is available for sale or licensing from LIST OF WHOLESALERS.

I have attached the marketing plan, a link to my book in electronic format, and an informational sheet for you to review.

Best,
YOUR NAME

To download a free editable Word template, visit NewShelves.com/indieauthors.

eBooks and Audiobooks in Library Systems

Digital lending is booming, and libraries are at the forefront. If you want your eBook or audiobook in libraries, you need to work with platforms they trust.

For eBooks, OverDrive (via Libby) is the gold standard. Hoopla is popular too, especially because it offers instant access to patrons. Bibliotheca (cloud Library) has solid reach in public and academic libraries alike.

Distributors like Draft2Digital and PublishDrive can get your eBooks into these systems. For audiobooks, Voices by INaudio is your best bet.

Each time your book is borrowed, you get paid a small royalty. But more importantly, you gain exposure to new readers who might never have found you otherwise.

Building Library Relationships

Start where you live. Local libraries are more likely to support local authors, especially those who show up with professionalism and a willingness to participate.

Offer to do a book talk, join a panel, or lead a workshop. Ask about community reading programs or author showcases. Be the kind of author who brings value, not just a sales pitch.

From there, build out. Contact other libraries in your county, state, or genre niche. Keep a spreadsheet. Follow up (nicely). Grow your presence over time. If librarians start recognizing your name in their inboxes—and your readers start requesting your book—you're on the right path.

Track your success using WorldCat.org, which shows where your book is shelved across global library systems.

The Library Strategy That Works

Libraries don't expect perfection, but they do expect you to act like a pro. Make your book easy to buy, easy to catalog, and easy to say "yes" to.

This isn't about overnight results. It's about layering opportunities until they become momentum. One library turns into five. Five turns into a regional purchase. Then a book club pick. Then a speaking invitation.

And all of that started because you treated your library strategy like a real part of your business plan.

For indie authors willing to think beyond launch day, libraries aren't just a nice-to-have. They're a secret weapon. A career builder. A legacy-maker. And one of the smartest, slowest, most satisfying ways to grow your reach without spending a fortune.

Now go earn your shelf space. It's waiting for you.

PART V

Scaling Your Author Career

CHAPTER 26

DIY PR vs. Hiring a Publicist

So you've got a book. You've built your platform. You've done your launch. Maybe you've even dipped your toes into advertising. Now you're wondering, should I hire a publicist? Or can I do this myself?

As an indie author, you wear a lot of hats. You're the writer, publisher, marketer, and yes, sometimes even your own publicist. When the time comes to grow your book's reach beyond your immediate audience, publicity can help. But deciding whether to hire a professional or do it yourself requires a clear-eyed look at your goals, budget, and timeline.

Publicity is not about instant sales. It's about visibility, credibility, and building the kind of third-party attention that enhances everything else you're doing to promote your book.

What a Publicist Can Offer

A qualified publicist works to connect you with media gatekeepers (podcast hosts, journalists, bloggers, producers, and event coordinators) who have the platforms to amplify your message. They pitch stories, arrange interviews, help shape your narrative, and ensure your presentation is media-ready. They also help you identify angles that connect your book with news cycles, seasonal features, or cultural conversations.

However, even the best publicist can't guarantee coverage. They can't guarantee ROI, either. Publicity is about planting seeds, not harvesting sales.

A publicist is not a substitute for your ongoing marketing plan. They don't run your ads, grow your email list, or manage your platform. They're part of your team—not the whole engine.

When Hiring Makes Sense

Hiring a publicist can be a smart move if your book has a timely or newsworthy hook, you're building a personal brand, or you're seeking regional or national media attention. It's also useful if you're looking to establish yourself as an expert or speaker beyond the book.

However, it's rarely cheap. A reputable publicity campaign can cost between $5,000 and $10,000 or more, and that doesn't include travel, copies of your book, or other promotional expenses. Publicists also expect their authors to be available and responsive to interview opportunities.

Before hiring anyone, do your research. Ask what media outlets they pitch to, what kind of results they've achieved for similar authors, and what a typical campaign includes. Beware of any publicist who guarantees coverage, lacks publishing experience, or adds on endless charges for basic services.

The DIY Option

Plenty of indie authors handle their own publicity—and do it well. With a smart plan, a polished presentation, and a dose of persistence, you can secure meaningful coverage without spending thousands.

Start by creating a simple, professional digital press kit. It should include your author bio, headshot, book description, cover image, purchase links, and contact info. Keep it clean and easy to read.

Next, identify relevant media outlets. Focus on smaller, accessible targets that match up with your book's audience. This might include local newspapers, radio stations, community blogs, podcasts, or newsletters that cover topics related to your book's themes.

Write a short, compelling pitch email for each contact. Personalize it. Explain why your book is a good fit for their audience right now. Then follow up once or twice, respectfully.

Writing Your Own Press Release

One of the simplest and most affordable DIY publicity tools is the press release. A press release is a short, formal announcement—typically 300 to 500 words—meant to alert media outlets to a newsworthy event, like a book launch, award, or tie-in with current events.

For indie authors, a well-crafted press release can help build awareness, attract media attention, and establish credibility. It's especially helpful for getting local or niche media coverage and can be repurposed for your website, bookstore outreach, or email list.

If you're new to press releases, start with a proven structure:

- A compelling headline

- A short summary paragraph

- Key details about the book and its relevance

- Author background

- Publication and purchasing information

- Contact information

Download a free press release template at NewShelves.com/indieauthors.

Once it's written, post the press release on your website, include it in your media kit, and send it directly to local news outlets, libraries, and bookstores. You can also use a press release distribution service. There are budget-friendly options that start around $50, which can help get your announcement in front of journalists and news syndicates.

Manage Your Expectations

Whether you do it yourself or hire a professional, it's important to keep your expectations realistic. Publicity is rarely the source of a dramatic sales spike. What it does offer is credibility; what marketers call social proof. When a trusted media outlet features your book, even briefly, it signals to others that your work is worth attention.

That credibility can boost your discoverability, help win over bookstores, and strengthen your author platform. It may also open doors to future opportunities, like speaking engagements or guest columns. Publicity won't replace your marketing plan, but when layered on top of a strong platform, it adds momentum.

You're Still in Charge

At the end of the day, even if you work with a professional, you are the face of your book. You are the one who will show up for interviews, respond to emails, and follow up with leads. Publicity is a powerful tool, but it only works if you use it well— and continue building your platform in the background.

The good news? Indie authors are used to leading the charge. You've already brought your book into the world. Taking a few more steps to share it through media outreach is just another way to amplify your hard work.

Whether you invest in a campaign or bootstrap your way through podcasts and local newspapers, remember that every bit of visibility counts. And while you may not see instant sales from a media mention, you're building the kind of long-term recognition that leads to lasting success.

CHAPTER 27

Long-Term Marketing Strategies

If you've launched your book and feel a little like Wile E. Coyote suspended mid-air, legs spinning above the canyon floor, congratulations. You've just entered the phase most authors dread, misunderstand, or ignore entirely: long-term marketing.

For many authors, the launch period comes with a surge of energy: email blasts, social media sprints, a few podcast appearances, maybe even some advertising. Then it's over. The calendar clears. The inbox empties. And sales begin their quiet, inevitable slide. Unless you intervene.

This chapter is not about the adrenaline rush of launch week. It's about building something that lasts. It's about longevity—about staying visible, valuable, and relevant long after your book is no longer "new." Most of all, it's about avoiding the cycle of burnout that has taken down far too many talented writers who didn't realize that launching a book is only the beginning.

The Myth of Momentum

Authors are often told that marketing is all about momentum. That's true, to a point, but too many interpret that as "you must go full speed, all the time." In reality, what readers and algorithms respond to isn't your bursts of energy. It's your ability to show up consistently. Marketing isn't a sprint. It's not even a marathon. It's more like tending a garden.

That means building marketing systems that are small, steady, and sustainable. If you can maintain a baseline effort— an email per month, a weekly post, a low-budget ad—you are already outpacing the majority of authors who disappear after launch and wonder why their sales died.

This isn't just about discipline. It's about survival. Burnout is a career killer. A long-term marketing strategy gives you the tools to stay in the game (and maybe even enjoy the process) without sacrificing your creative energy.

Consistency Beats Brilliance

If your plan is to post feverishly for one week and then disappear into the woods until your next book, you're setting yourself up to fail. Success in publishing doesn't come from one-time hype. It comes from repeatable action.

One thoughtful email a month beats ten frantic ones in a week. One reader-focused post is more effective than a dozen desperate "Buy my book!" blasts. A modest but consistent ad budget outperforms a single weekend blitz. Your job isn't to go viral. Your job is to keep showing up with value. Think drip campaign, not fire hose.

Building Evergreen Systems

What separates authors who flail from those who flourish is their ability to build evergreen systems—marketing tools and strategies that work even when they aren't actively pushing buttons.

These systems don't replace human connection, but they create a reliable framework for discovery, nurture, and sales.

A reader discovers you through a podcast or ad. They sign up for a free story or bonus chapter. They get a welcome sequence that introduces who you are, what you write, and why they should care. They get value-packed emails like behind-the-scenes content, recommendations, sneak peeks. Every few emails, you make a pitch. They buy. They stay.

That's a funnel. Simple, repeatable, scalable. Tools like Kit, MailerLite, and BookFunnel make it possible even if you can't code your way out of a Word document. You don't need to be a tech genius. You need a plan.

A Closer Look: The Funnel Flow

1. **Discovery:** Social posts, interviews, ads, guest content, or SEO

2. **Lead Magnet:** Offer a short story, sample chapters, checklist, or guide

3. **Signup:** They exchange their email address for the freebie

4. **Welcome Sequence:** Automated emails that deliver value and establish your brand

5. **Ongoing Nurture:** Regular, helpful, non-annoying emails

6. **Soft Pitches:** Timed promos, discounts, and endorsements

7. **Loyalty and Conversion:** They become a buyer. A fan. An advocate.

It's not magic. But once it's running, it sure feels like it.

Smart Facebook Ads: Not Just for Launches

Paid ads aren't just for launch week, and Facebook Ads, in particular, can be one of the most powerful evergreen tools in your long-term marketing system. When done right, they don't just sell books; they build audience, test messaging, and keep your funnel flowing ... even while you sleep.

To be clear: this isn't about dumping $500 into a boosted post and hoping the algorithm sends readers your way. It's about treating ads like a business investment ... an investment that grows as your knowledge (and results) grow.

I'm a big fan of Facebook ads. You can use them to build awareness, grow your following, market a current book, or even drive sign-ups to your funnel or mailing list. But only if you stop trusting Facebook's default settings.

Don't Boost Blind

Yes, boosting a post is technically an ad. But that bright little blue button? It's designed to spend your money fast—not wisely. Facebook defaults to automatic settings like "get more messages" (why?) and "Advantage Audience," which sounds like a good thing ... until it blows through your budget trying to figure out who your audience *might* be.

> *"Let Facebook choose," they say. "We have your best interest in mind." It's lies. It's all lies.*

Instead of letting Facebook decide, click "Change" when setting up your boost and select an actual goal:

- **Get More Engagement:** Use this when you're posting memes, behind-the-scenes content, or cover reveals and want likes, shares, and comments to grow your author page and presence.

- **Get More Website Visitors:** Perfect when you're sending people to your Amazon page or website, especially with an Amazon Attribution link to track ROI.

- **Skip "Get More Leads" and "Get More Calls."** You're not running a call center or selling car insurance here. You're selling books.

Also: please, change the call-to-action button. "Send Message" is rarely what you want. Instead, use:

- **Learn More:** Great for reader curiosity with less pressure.

- **Shop Now:** Best when directing traffic to your Amazon or Shopify page.

- **No Button:** Totally fine if it's a pure engagement post.

Build Your Audience the Right Way

Be wary of jumping into ads with Facebook's Advantage Audience setting. Instead, create an audience manually to teach the algorithms who your ideal reader is, and then consider using the Advantage Audience later once it's "trained."

What does that mean in plain English?

Don't let Facebook spray your ad across random regions and call it a day. Build an audience:

- **Location:** Stick to your actual sales platform. Sending UK readers to amazon.com? Waste of money.

- **Age & Gender:** Be honest about your ideal reader and demographic. Most genres lean toward specific reader segments.

- **Interests:** Target readers who like BookBub, Goodreads, or specific comp authors. Big names like "Colleen Hoover" or "Jodi Picoult" work. Smaller ones may not show up.

If you're selling a book in women's fiction, for example, try targeting US women ages 45–65+ who follow BookBub and read authors in your niche. That's more useful than "people who like your page," especially if your page only has 73 followers and two of them are your sisters.

Start Small, Spend Smart

You don't need to drop a car payment on Facebook ads when you're just getting started ... And I recommend that you don't. Rather, start testing ads with a $2–$3/day budget, run the ad for at least 10–14 days (Facebook needs time to optimize), and track what happens. For engagement posts, you might get clicks for $0.01–$0.03 each. For direct-to-Amazon campaigns, a good cost-per-click (CPC) is $0.10–$0.30.

And double-check whether your budget is daily or lifetime before hitting publish. A $100/day ad that runs for a week is not the same thing as a $100 total campaign. Ask me how I know.

Test Creative That Works

Forget fancy book trailers or polished cover graphics. Some of the cheapest, highest-performing ads use memes as the visual component of the ad creative.

In one recent campaign, a spicy romance meme brought in 92 clicks for just $12. That's $0.13 per click, and the click-through rate was close to 10%. That kind of performance is hard to beat.

Why do memes work? Because they're native to the platform. They feel fun, not salesy. And if they're relatable, people share them—extending your reach for free.

> *Pro Tip: Match your meme to your genre.*
> *Spicy romance? Use sass. Historical fiction?*
> *Try bookish trivia or elegant humor. Sci-fi?*
> *Niche in-jokes are gold.*

Check the Right Metrics

High reach means nothing if no one clicks.

Watch your click-through rate (CTR). If it's at least 2.5%, the CTR is decent. 5% or over is strong indicating that your ad creative is aligning with your targeted audience. Track cost per click (CPC), too. Keeping that under $0.15 is ideal for most book ads and you definitely don't want to be spending more than $0.30 per click. Monitor frequency and demographics to see who's actually engaging. And always ask yourself: Is this ad doing what I asked it to do?

Marketing without tracking is like throwing darts in the dark. You might hit something eventually, but it won't be efficient, and it certainly won't be repeatable.

Use what you learn. Drop what doesn't work. Scale what does.

Facebook Ads Quick Checklist

- Choose the right ad objective (Engagement or Website Visitors)

- Build a custom audience (age, location, interests)

- Use a compelling visual (meme or clean promo graphic)

- Update your CTA button (usually Learn More or Shop Now)

- Set a modest budget ($2–$5/day) for 10–14 days

- Use Amazon Attribution if sending to a retail link

- Track CTR and CPC weekly

- Tweak, test, repeat

Used correctly, Facebook Ads don't just boost your post; they boost your career. So don't be afraid to give them a try.

Relationships, Not Just Reach

Long-term sales come from long-term relationships. While ads can bring in new eyeballs, it's your email list that turns those eyeballs into actual readers.

Don't treat your list like a billboard. Treat it like a conversation. Share what you're reading, working on, or thinking about. Pull back the curtain. Invite engagement. Relevance is earned through authenticity and consistency.

And while social media can help, it shouldn't own your relationship with readers. Choose platforms that fit your strengths. Show up as a human, not a headline machine. Focus less on followers and more on actual connection.

Diversify Where You Show Up

Not every reader is scrolling Instagram. Some are listening to podcasts, reading guest posts, or showing up to events. Don't limit your visibility to your comfort zone.

Be a podcast guest. Offer a free class to a local library. Submit an article to a blog in your niche. Every new audience is a new opportunity to build trust. And trust leads to loyalty.

> *The goal is not to be everywhere. It's to be somewhere meaningful ... and to make that presence count.*

Collaborations and Speaking Gigs

You don't have to do this alone. Partner with other authors for giveaways, newsletter swaps, or joint launches. Share your audience. Share the spotlight. Everybody wins.

Pitch yourself as a speaker. Book clubs, schools, conferences, and community centers are always looking for speakers with something valuable to say. You don't need a shocking headline. You need a story that matters.

Avoid Burnout

If your marketing plan requires you to be everywhere, do everything, and post constantly, you're headed straight for burnout.

Start batching. Reuse your best content. Take breaks after major campaigns. Plan your output the same way you plan your writing. And if it's not working? Cut it. Marketing should feel like growth, not erosion.

Know What's Working

If you want your book sales to grow, you need to know—without guessing—what's actually moving the needle. And the key to figuring that out is to use the data.

> *Your job is not just to do the marketing, it's to understand whether it's working.*

If something isn't working, kill it. Stop pouring money or time into tactics that don't convert. If something *is* working, lean in. Double down. Scale.

And no, this doesn't mean you have to become a spreadsheet wizard. But if you have no idea where your readers are coming from, you're not running a business, you're playing a guessing game. A quick glance at your sales dashboard, ad performance, or email metrics every week can tell you a lot.

So check in. Look at the numbers. Learn the story they're telling you. Then tweak, test, and evolve. That's how authors turn scattered sales into strategic growth.

Play the Long Game

This is not a one-book business. It's a long-haul strategy. Marketing that matters is marketing that sticks. It doesn't shout. It resonates. And it builds something that lasts.

The authors who win aren't always the loudest or the luckiest. They're the ones who stay in the game. They outlast the algorithm. They show up, consistently, with something worth saying.

So stay in the game. Keep building. Keep testing. Keep showing up.

Your book isn't the end. It's just the start of your brand.

CHAPTER 28

Scaling Up: Turning One Book into a Career

Publishing your first book is a landmark achievement. But in this industry, a single book is not a business. It's a seed. Whether it grows into a hobby, a side hustle, or a full-scale career depends on what you do next.

Scaling up as an indie author is not about writing faster or working harder. It's about working smarter. It's about building systems, leveraging assets, and thinking like a publisher. In this chapter, we're not talking about getting another book out the door. We're talking about building a sustainable, diversified, and scalable author business that supports your long-term goals.

This chapter is where we shift from author to entrepreneur. From book hustler to intellectual property strategist. From "Yay, I hit publish!" to "Now how do I make this thing scale without having a nervous breakdown?"

Welcome to the business of being an author.

Stop Thinking in Single Titles

If you're still thinking about your work as one standalone book, you're playing the game on beginner mode with a broken controller.

Readers binge. If they like your first book and can't find another, they'll forget you existed by next Tuesday. Retailers reward authors who release consistently. Algorithms nudge authors with deep catalogs. And momentum only happens when there's something for it to build on.

You don't need to crank out a book every 90 days or live chained to Scrivener. But if you want a real career, you do need a backlist.

Whether it's a trilogy, a series of connected standalones, or nonfiction books that hammer home your core promise, the goal is the same. Create a body of work that builds trust, drives repeat sales, and gives your marketing more than one note to play.

Turn Systems Into Infrastructure

Back in Chapter 27, we walked through how to build an evergreen sales funnel. Now it's time to step back and see it for what it really is: infrastructure.

Funnels, onboarding sequences, and lead magnets are not just marketing tactics. They are the framework that supports your publishing business. When your books, ads, emails, and backend are aligned and automated, you're no longer flying by the seat of your pants. You're running a business.

Scaling means reinforcing that infrastructure so you can publish more, market better, and reach further—without losing your mind or sleep schedule.

Your Book Is Not Just a Book

You didn't *just* write a book. You created an asset. And assets should work harder than you do.

That book can be an eBook, paperback, hardcover, audiobook, large print edition, workbook, or bundle. It can be sold direct, licensed to a foreign publisher, turned into a keynote, or expanded into a paid course.

But only if you stop thinking like a writer and start acting like a publisher.

Got a nonfiction book? You might be sitting on a curriculum. A corporate workshop. A coaching offer. A lead generator for consulting clients.

Writing fiction? You can still teach. Craft, world-building, writing habits ... someone out there wants what you know. That short story you cut in edits? Great bonus content. That subplot that didn't fit? Perfect lead magnet for readers. You don't need new material. You need better packaging.

Monetize the Rights You Already Own

If you're only selling eBooks and print-on-demand paperbacks, you're playing with a tiny fraction of your book's potential. You own the rights. Use them.

- **Audiobooks** are booming. Produce it yourself or license it, but don't leave it on the table. Tools like ACX and Voices by INaudio, along with platforms like Spotify and Chirp, are opening new paths every day.

- **Foreign rights and translations** open entire global markets. Germany, France, and Italy are especially open to quality indie books. You can license translation rights to foreign publishers or commission and publish yourself. Either way, hire professionals. A bad translation is worse than no translation.

- **Special editions** can also create long-tail revenue. Large print for libraries. Deluxe hardcovers for superfans. Kickstarter campaigns. Anthologies. Don't wait for someone to ask you. Package your work. Pitch it. License it. Expand it.

- **Create Courses** and expand your reach. If your book solves a problem or teaches a concept, it can absolutely become a course. Stop telling yourself you need a PhD or a studio setup. You need clarity, structure, and a platform.

You already wrote the outline. It's in your table of contents. Turn it into videos. Add checklists. Sell it through Teachable or Podia. Host a workshop. Run a live cohort. Layer it into a newsletter-based course. Or start with a free version and upsell into deeper content.

Nonfiction That Builds a Business

Not all indie authors are chasing book royalties alone. For many nonfiction writers—especially consultants, coaches, and entrepreneurs—the real win isn't on the bestseller list. It's behind the scenes: building authority, generating leads, and growing a business that lasts.

That's the power of nonfiction in the indie space. Done right, a book becomes more than a product. It's a platform.

CASE STUDY: PAT FLYNN

Growing a Business through Self-Published Nonfiction

Pat Flynn is best known as the voice behind *Smart Passive Income*, a wildly successful blog and podcast that's helped thousands of people launch online businesses. But in 2016, Flynn took his next big step: he self-published *Will It Fly?*, a book that helps readers test and validate business ideas before launching.

This wasn't a random content repack. It was a smart business move, and a strategic expansion of his brand.

Built for His Audience

Flynn didn't write *Will It Fly?* for strangers. He wrote it for the people already tuning into his podcast, reading his blog, and following his work. The book was born from the questions his audience was already asking and it became the next logical step in their journey.

It wasn't just content. It was connection.

Self-Published on Purpose

Flynn had the platform to land a traditional deal. But he chose to self-publish so he could retain control, speed up production, and keep more of the profits. The result? A bestselling book that fit seamlessly into his business funnel, instead of bending to a publisher's timeline.

The Business Strategy Behind the Book

Flynn didn't just launch a book. He extended his brand.

- **Email List Growth:** Readers who bought the book were invited to download bonus tools—capturing email addresses and building deeper engagement.

- **Consulting and Courses:** The book wasn't the final product. It was the entry point to Flynn's paid offerings: online courses, webinars, and coaching.

- **Speaking and Media:** The credibility from publishing a high-quality book landed him speaking gigs, podcast appearances, and media features in outlets like the *New York Times* and *Forbes*.

- **Reader Investment:** By documenting the book's creation process and inviting feedback, Flynn turned readers into co-creators—and ambassadors.

Flynn didn't just write a book and hope for sales. He wrote a book that served his audience, expanded his brand, and generated long-term ROI across multiple business channels.

Results That Compound

Since publishing *Will It Fly?*, Flynn has used the book as:

- A lead magnet
- A credibility booster
- A funnel for higher-ticket products and services

It continues to sell years later, not because of ad spend or algorithm luck, but because it works within a larger, sustainable business strategy.

Flynn's journey proves that a nonfiction book can do more

than fill a shelf; it can fill a pipeline. By treating his book as a tool, not just a product, he expanded his business, deepened his authority, and created new revenue streams without chasing traditional publishing validation.

And while Flynn's story centers on nonfiction, the principle applies across genres. Fiction authors might not create courses but your stories, characters, and process can still become springboards for connection, creativity, and income.

CASE STUDY: BARBARA HINSKE

Building a Fiction Career with Strategic Scaling

Barbara Hinske didn't stumble into success—she built it brick by brick. A former lawyer turned full-time writer, Hinske made the shift to self-publishing with clear intention and a strategic mindset. Her novel *The Christmas Club* began as a heartfelt, independently published holiday story. But with smart branding, strong writing, and consistent marketing, it snowballed into something far bigger: a Hallmark Channel adaptation, a thriving fanbase, and a full-blown fiction brand.

Here's what Hinske did right:

- **Genre Mastery:** She knew her audience and wrote to their expectations without being formulaic. Her books deliver warmth, emotional connection, and the kind of stories readers return to year after year.

- **Consistent Publishing:** Hinske didn't stop at one book. She released multiple titles in connected genres, building a reliable reading experience. Readers didn't just buy one book, they returned for the next (and the next after that).

- **Professional Production:** Her covers, editing, and interior formatting never screamed "self-published." They looked like any traditionally published bestseller, and that professionalism paid off.

- **Author Partnerships and Promotion:** Hinske invested in expert marketing support and collaborated with professionals who helped get her books in front of the right audience, including targeted outreach, advertising, and book club engagement.

- **Rights Expansion:** The Hallmark Channel deal didn't just land in her lap. Her book was written and packaged in a way that made it ideal for film adaptation, and she actively sought to make connections that might lead to a book to film adaptation.

Today, Hinske is not just an indie author; she's a fiction entrepreneur. Her catalog keeps growing, her audience keeps coming back, and her stories have reached readers far beyond what a single book could have done.

Her story shows that fiction authors can scale just as effectively as their nonfiction peers. The key? Treating your writing like a business and your books like a brand.

Build Systems or Drown in Admin

Once you've published a few books, you'll start noticing the chaos creep in. Updating files, managing back matter, fixing links, launching ads, onboarding ARC readers—every task repeats. And multiplies.

The only solution? Systems.

Document your processes. Create SOPs. Automate what you can. Outsource where it makes sense. Your job is not to become a project manager or tech support. Your job is to lead. Write. Publish. Scale.

Even if you're a team of one, you need a strategy that respects your time.

Future-Proof Your Author Career

Relying on one book, one platform, or one income stream is like building a house on a single pillar. It might hold for a while, but it's not built for the long haul. The authors who thrive over time are the ones who diversify across formats, platforms, audiences, and revenue models. This isn't about doing everything. It's about creating a resilient, flexible author business that can grow with you and support your long-term goals.

Multiple streams of income don't just provide protection. They give you options, leverage, and breathing room. They allow you to take creative risks, experiment with new ideas, and stay in the game even when one channel slows down.

Let's look at a modern indie author who has done exactly that.

CASE STUDY: ELIZABETH STEPHENS

Blending Indie and Traditional Success with Strategic Diversification

Elizabeth Stephens, whom Amy Collins also mentioned in the Foreword of this book, is a hybrid author who has built her career through variety—in content, publishing models, and income streams. Her breakout title *Taken to Voraxia* became a self-publishing hit, gaining widespread attention among romance and sci-fi fans.

Instead of picking one lane, Elizabeth continued publishing independently while also pursuing opportunities with traditional publishers. She leaned into direct-to-consumer marketing, learned the platforms, tested strategies, and kept what worked. She took the parts of publishing that felt murky or inaccessible, rolled up her sleeves, and made them hers.

That dual strategy paid off. She licensed translation rights for her self-published titles and signed a deal with Amazon's Montlake imprint for her novel *All Superheroes Need PR*. At the same time, she kept releasing books under her own brand, maintaining creative control and a strong reader connection.

Here's how Elizabeth has future-proofed her author business:

- **Multiple publishing channels:** She continues to self-publish while also working with a traditional publisher, expanding her reach without giving up ownership.

- **Rights licensing:** By securing foreign rights deals, she opens new markets and income streams beyond English-speaking readers.

- **Genre variety:** Her books span multiple romance subgenres, appealing to a broader range of fans without diluting her voice.

- **Consistent output:** Regular releases keep readers engaged and ensure her backlist continues to generate revenue.

- **Strong reader engagement:** Elizabeth actively connects

with her audience through newsletters and social media, building loyalty across all her titles.

Elizabeth's approach shows that success isn't about finding the one perfect path. It's about building a portfolio of assets (books, readers, rights, and platforms) that support each other and give your career staying power.

Diversifying your publishing efforts isn't a backup plan. It's a growth strategy. Whether that means licensing foreign rights, experimenting with new genres, or exploring both indie and traditional routes, the more options you have, the more control you keep.

Scale With Intention

Scaling isn't just about growth. It's about intentional growth. Smart authors don't chase every opportunity; they evaluate what fits their goals, strengths, and audience.

So build a backlist. Monetize your IP. Track your numbers. Protect your energy. And make the shift from solo indie author to publishing CEO.

You already did the hard part. Now it's time to build something that lasts.

CHAPTER 29

Ready to Win at Self-Publishing?

You made it.

You've walked through the complexities of indie publishing—dodging scams, mastering metadata, navigating distribution, managing production, and facing down the unpredictable beast known as book marketing.

Take a breath.

Now exhale, because here's the final and most important piece of tough love: what you do after this chapter matters more than anything you've just read.

This is not the finish line. This is the starting block.

You now have the tools, the systems, and the strategic framework. You've seen what works, what doesn't, and what separates a self-published book from a professionally published one. You know the difference between treating your writing like a hobby and running your career like a business.

Now it's time to move forward. Intentionally.

No One Owes You Sales

Not Amazon. Not your readers. Not your friends or family.

Writing a great book is not the final achievement. It is the minimum requirement. If you want reach, visibility, or consistent sales, you will need to earn it through strategy, professionalism, and consistent action.

Some authors get lucky. Most do not. The ones who succeed are not the luckiest or the loudest. They're the ones who keep showing up. They stay in the game long enough to understand how it works. They invest. They adapt. They get better.

And they keep going.

The Difference Between Struggling and Successful Authors

It's not talent. It's not budget. It's not who you know.

It's action.

Strategic. Consistent. Imperfect. Action.

Successful authors are not waiting for perfect timing or a perfect plan. They apply what they know. They fix what breaks. They build as they go. They treat missteps as tuition.

You can revise a cover. Rewrite a blurb. Rebuild your platform. Relaunch a book.

But you cannot succeed if you never start.

Show Up for Your Book

No one can advocate for your book like you can. You are the voice of your brand, the anchor of your audience, and the most credible advocate for your work.

That doesn't mean doing everything alone. But it does mean owning the role of publisher—and taking responsibility for how your book enters the world.

Readers are not motivated by how hard you worked. They are moved by what your book offers. Focus on that and lead with value.

> *Be visible. Be confident. Be ready to stand behind your work.*

Launch Week Is Not Your Career

A strong launch is valuable, but it's not the foundation of your success.

Most bestselling indie authors did not build careers on launch spikes. They built them on backlists, reader loyalty, and long-term discoverability.

Your goal is not a viral moment. Your goal is sustained relevance.

Write the next book. Then the next one. Create a body of work that builds momentum over time. Publishing success is cumulative, not instant.

You Don't Have to Do Everything

Ignore the noise that says you must be everywhere, all at once.

You do not need to be on every platform, run every ad type, attend every event, or master every trend. You only need a strategy that is sustainable, aligned with your goals, and consistent enough to gain traction.

Choose what works. Double down on what matters. Let go of what doesn't serve your vision.

Momentum comes from focus, not frenzy.

You're Not Behind

It's easy to feel like you're late to the game. You're not.

Whether you're on your first book or your fifteenth, your timeline is valid. Success in publishing is not a race, and it's never too late to start building a meaningful career.

Ignore the comparisons. They are distractions.

The only timeline that matters is your own. Stay on it.

Keep Learning. Keep Building. Keep Writing.

You are no longer just a writer. You are a publisher. You are an entrepreneur. You are a strategist.

The industry will keep changing. Algorithms will shift. Tools will evolve. But your ability to adapt, *that* is your competitive advantage.

Whatever your next step is—whether it's refining your backlist, improving your metadata, or launching a new series—know this: you already have what most people lack.

You took action.

What Now? Your Final Checklist

Use this as your next-step framework. Pick a few. Prioritize. Move forward.

Author Business & Infrastructure

- Revisit your publishing setup: metadata, formats, pricing, and availability.

- Clarify your imprint, LLC or DBA status, and update platform accounts.

Marketing & Growth

- Build or improve your lead magnet and welcome sequence.
- Strengthen your author platform: website, email list, social visibility.
- Establish a review-building strategy.

Sustainability & Focus

- Identify your primary revenue channels (retail, direct, events, speaking).
- Eliminate tasks that are draining your time without delivering results.
- Create a content calendar that lines up with your publishing goals.

Long-Term Planning

- Map your next three titles.
- Develop a 12-month marketing plan.
- Track and review your numbers regularly: royalties, ad spend, list growth.

Final Word

You will face setbacks. You will receive criticism. You will second-guess yourself.

Keep going anyway.

This book has given you a roadmap. But a roadmap only

works if you use it. The indie authors who succeed are not the ones who read the most books about publishing. They are the ones who take what they've learned and apply it.

Write the next book. Launch smarter. Market intentionally. Treat your writing like the business it is.

You've got what it takes.

I'll see you out there—on the bestseller lists, at bookstore signings, in the speaking circuit, and on the shelf between some of the greats.

Now go take over the publishing world. One chapter at a time.

Glossary of Terms

Ad Creative The visual and written elements of an advertisement, including images, graphics, headlines, and copy, designed to capture attention and persuade an audience to take action.

Advanced Reader Copy (ARC) A prepublication copy of a book released before the final printing. A publisher will send ARCs out for marketing and publicity purposes to generate interest in the book.

Agent A professional within the book industry who represents an author and the author's work to publishers.

Back Matter Printed material that follows the main text of a book. Back matter may include, but is not limited to, an appendix, afterword, and index.

Backlist A list of a publisher's titles that are still in print but not recently published.

Bleed Printing to the very edge of the paper. Often the paper is cut to ensure that the print does not stop short of the edge.

Buyer A person or group of people responsible for choosing and purchasing the books that a retailer will sell to the public.

Chain A large corporation that owns several bookstores under one name.

Consignment A sales model where the author provides books to a store and only gets paid if they sell.

Co-op A co-operative. Advertising produced by a bookseller, the cost of which is shared by the publisher.

Copy Editor A professional within the book industry who edits a manuscript for grammar, spelling, word usage, style, and clarity of writing.

Copy Editing A form of editing that focuses on grammar, spelling, word usage, style, and clarity of writing.

Design The arrangement of text, illustrations, page numbers, running heads, margins, front matter and back matter, as well as the designation of fonts and graphics, to create a book's layout.

Digital Printing A printing technology that is able to print a book directly from a computer file.

Distribution The process of moving books into the retail market.

Distributor A company a publisher hires to handle the sales, warehousing, shipping, and billing of its books.

DPI Dots per inch. DPI refers to the degree of resolution determined by the number of dots printed per linear inch. The higher the DPI, the greater the resolution and quality.

EAN Bar Code The translation of an ISBN into barcode form for electronic scanning.

Editor A professional within the book industry who evaluates a manuscript as a whole and edits the manuscript for organization, tone, consistency, clarity, flow, and logic. The editor will rework or rewrite the text as necessary and offer suggestions to the author, requesting that he or she flesh out an idea, clarify an issue, and/or resolve faulty logic. Sometimes called a developmental editor, structural editor, substantive editor, or content editor.

Font A complete set of characters available in a specific size and style of typeface.

Front Matter Printed material that precedes the main text of a book. Front matter may include, but is not limited to, a copyright page, title page, table of contents, dedication, and introduction.

Frontlist A list of a publisher's new titles that are being released in the current season.

Fulfillment The activities involved in processing an order, including invoicing, accounts receivable, collections, shipping and handling, warehousing, and maintaining customer, sales, and inventory records.

Genre A specific category of literature. Examples of genres include romance, science fiction, mystery, true crime, etc.

Gutter The white space of the inner margins where two pages come together in a two-page spread.

ISBN International Standard Book Number. A series of thirteen digits specific to the book industry that identifies the group or country of the publication, publisher, and title.

Layout The overall design of a book.

Lead Magnet Sometimes referred to as a "reader magnet" in the book marketing world, a lead magnet is a free resource offered to readers in exchange for their email address. Common examples include a short story, sample chapter, checklist, or exclusive bonus content.

Margins The white space around the main body of text on a page.

Marketing A process of advertising and promoting an author's work.

Offset Printing A high-quality printing technique in which an image is transferred from a plate to a rubber cylinder and then onto paper.

One-page Title Information Sheet A part of a sales kit that includes a book's pertinent information. A title information sheet includes: ISBN, title, subtitle, author's name, author's bio, author's hometown, 100-word description of book, order contact information, book category, retail price, page count, trim size, ship date, publication date, format, print run, co-op and advertising budget, title and ISBN of previous books by author or in the series, title and ISBN of books similar to featured book.

Orphan The first line of a paragraph that appears alone at the bottom of a page, leaving it disconnected from the rest of the text.

PDF Portable document format. An electronic document format that allows for the distribution of a digital file that maintains all the elements of the original. Developed by Adobe.

POD Print on demand. A business model using digital printing technology that allows books to be printed in small quantities, even one at a time, permitting publishers to print books as they are ordered.

Positioning Statement A 100-word statement that outlines for a potential buyer the reasons why a book will be of interest to their clients. This statement exists to talk about the potential market for a book and how the publisher plans to reach that market.

Press Release A written announcement of a book and/or author sent to the media in hopes of creating publicity.

Print Run The number of copies printed for a publisher at one time.

Proofreader A professional within the book industry who checks a typeset book for errors in text and design and makes corrections as necessary.

Proofreading The process of checking a typeset book for errors in text and design. Often, proofreading involves checking the typeset book against the copy edited manuscript to ensure that all changes have been incorporated into the final set.

Publicity Media exposure of a book.

Resolution The clarity and quality of an image, measured in DPI.

Returns Unsold copies of a book returned to a publisher for a full refund.

Sales Kit A package of informative material used to persuade buyers to purchase a book. A sales kit includes, but is not limited to, a cover, a complete outline of the book, positioning and marketing statements, a few sample chapters, and a one-page sheet listing all the book's pertinent information.

Self-publishing The publishing of a work by the work's author.

Street Team A group of readers who volunteer to read your book before publication and help promote it, often by leaving reviews and spreading the word around launch.

Table of Contents A list of the divisions of a book with corresponding page numbers. Divisions may include chapter numbers, chapter titles, part numbers, part titles, and/or section/subhead titles.

Target Audience The intended readers of a book. A target audience is a specific group defined by characteristics such as demographic, age, gender, lifestyle, etc.

Trim Size The dimensions of a finished book.

Warehousing The process of storing and stocking an inventory of books.

Wholesaler A company that buys books at a deep discount and warehouses them for orders from bookstores, libraries, and online retailers.

Widow The last line of a paragraph that appears alone at the top of a new page, creating awkward white space and disrupting readability.

About the Author

Keri-Rae Barnum is the owner and CEO of New Shelves Books, a full-service publishing consulting and book marketing agency. A leading expert in self-publishing and book marketing, she has helped hundreds of authors turn their writing into successful careers through strategic platform building, dynamic book launches, and innovative marketing campaigns.

With a deep understanding of what it truly takes to succeed in indie publishing, Keri is known for her no-nonsense approach to book marketing and author career growth. She works closely with both publishers and independent authors to enhance production, distribution, and visibility in bookstores, libraries, and digital platforms.

A sought-after international speaker, Keri shares her expertise at writing and publishing events, equipping authors with the tools they need to navigate the realities of self-publishing. Her passion for education and commitment to industry transparency make her an invaluable resource for writers who are ready to approach their publishing goals with strategy, persistence, and a business mindset.

Discover more about Keri and connect with her at www.NewShelves.com.

Learn More about Sibyl Writing
Craft Books and Courses

Sibylline
PRESS

Sibylline Press is proud to publish the brilliant work of women authors over 50. We are a woman-owned publishing company and, like our authors, represent women of a certain age.

How to Write Stunning Sentences • Living the Life: Writing Vivid, Memorable Characters • The Joys and Challenges of Revision: A Hands-on Approach to Forming and Finishing a Project for Publication • A Writer's Resolution: Setting Your Goals for the New Year • The Sound of Story—Finding, Crafting and Playing with Voice • 'Tude and Tone: How Attitude and Opinion Shape Page Turning Characters • Voice and POV: Shifting Perspectives, Shifting Voice • When the Character is You: Curating Voice in the Memoir or Essay • Voice Up Your Non-Fiction: How to Capture and Keep Reader Attention • Tone, Emotion and Mood: Controlling Your Readers' Feelings • The Sound of Story—Finding Crafting and Playing with Voice • Lyrical Writing For Plot-Forward Writers • Revising for Voice: Polishing This Key Element of Successful Writing • Experiments in Voice: Breaking Free From Usual Forms • Sound of Story: Voice and Tone Immersion • Looking to the Past: How to Research your Historical Fiction • Writing from Multiple Viewpoints • The Tough Love Publishing Intensive: Get Real. Get Ready. Get Published • Path to Publication • Are You Actually Ready to Publish? • Ask Us Anything — Live Publishing Strategy Q&A • One Book Won't Pay the Bills: Real Talk About Author Income, Career Growth, and Making It Work • Social Media for Authors: The Good, the Bad, and the Absolutely Necessary • Pitch Perfect: Sell Your Book to Bookstores, Libraries, and Gatekeepers • Understanding Rights and Licensing • Understanding the World of Book Publishing • Acquisitions for Noobs: How to get through the door! • On the Frontlines with Bookstores • Bookstore Presentation Coaching by an Expert

Learn more about our books and courses!

Books and Courses Designed for Writers

Sibylline Press is thrilled to introduce our new writing craft series paired with online writing courses.

Sibyl Writing Craft's 2026 courses include 30 different offerings taught by our instructors, each dedicated to different aspects of writing and the business of book publishing. Our instructors (we call them mentors) are women of a certain age with years of wisdom and experience and they include many of our partners at Sibylline Press. And yes, we are all writers as well.

Each year, as writers, we think about what we will accomplish in the coming year. We set our goals and revisit our ambitions. It may be to improve some aspect of our craft, to hone the work we have, to start something new, to achieve publication, or to jumpstart our author skills once published.

At Sibyl Writing Craft, we can revel with you at the sentence level or help you polish your manuscripts using the tools of voice, tone, character, and point of view, to name a few. We can assist with your revisions. We can walk you through the book industry and how it really works. We can shed light on how licensing and rights work or train you on social media. We can provide a road map for indie authors to capitalize on every opportunity. We can train you to present to bookstores. We know you will delight in our range offerings as much as we delighted in creating them.

Our courses are designed as Confabs, which are 75-minute informational talks on a topic, and the longer Labs, which provide more interactivity for participants on a given subject over three or more sessions. Each Confab or Lab comes with one of our Sibyl Writing Craft books on that subject and is taught by that author. Most Confabs and Labs take place on Zoom. Some take place in partner bookstores.

In addition to offering fabulous courses, we've got gifts. Upon enrollment in our Confabs or Labs this first year, you'll receive a complimentary copy of *A Writer's Resolution*. This writer's journal will help you plan your writing future.

We can't wait to collaborate with you on your writing and publishing journey. We are invested in your success as a writer. And as a book publisher, the team at Sibylline Press even hopes to see your best work in our submissions portal.

 **To learn more about our Confabs or Labs for the year, please see our catalog at sibyllinepress.com.**

Titles Coming in 2026

HOW TO WRITE
Stunning
SENTENCES
100 Simple Exercises
from Beloved Authors to
Improve Your Writing Style

NINA SCHUYLER

Stunning
SENTENCES
A Creative Writing Journal
with 80 Prompts from Beloved Writers
to Improve Your Writing Style

NINA SCHUYLER

THE
Sound
OF
Story
Developing **Voice and Tone** in Writing

JORDAN
ROSENFELD

Tough
Love
for **INDIE AUTHORS**
An Honest Look at What it Takes to
Win in Self-Publishing

KERI-RAE BARNUM
Foreword by **AMY COLLINS**

PLUS: *A Writer's Resolution: A Guided Journal for Realizing a Rewarding Writing Practice* By Christine Walker

www.ingramcontent.com/pod-product-compliance
Lightning Source LLC
Jackson TN
JSHW020205110126
96700JS00004B/5